THE HIGH WIND

BOOKS BY W.E. BUTTERWORTH

AIR EVAC
CRAZY TO RACE
FAST AND SMART
FAST GREEN CAR
GRAND PRIX DRIVER
HELICOPTER PILOT
MARTY AND THE MICRO-MIDGETS
REDLINE 7100
ROAD RACER
SOLDIERS ON HORSEBACK
STOCK CAR RACER
THE WHEEL OF A FAST CAR
RETURN TO RACING
THE HIGH WIND

THE HIGH WIND

The Story of NASCAR Racing

by W.E. BUTTERWORTH

With a Foreword by

PHILIP HOLMER

A W. W. NORTON BOOK

Published by

GROSSET & DUNLAP, INC.

New York

FOREWORD

Back in the late 40s when the rest of the nation was trying to figure out Harry Truman and the Brooklyn Dodgers, the sporting world of the South was experiencing a revolution — a nice, quiet upheaval whose roar could only be heard at the dusty little racetracks that dotted the Carolina countryside.

In 1948 the battered modified cars started on the beach at Daytona and then followed the High Wind to the north. For the first time, stock car racing was organized under the fledgling NASCAR banner. A year later, at Charlotte, N. C., the cyclone reappeared for the first Grand National race. Nine races composed the championship series that year, inauspicious for sure.

Then came Darlington. The supertrack — 1 3/8 miles forged out of a cotton field without blueprints. The High Wind took hold that Labor Day, 1950, and in six and a half hours the crest was ready to sweep the rest of the country.

Stock car racing moved from the infant to the adolescent stage in the next ten years, and then Bill France turned a swamp full of gators into Daytona International

Speedway. In the 60s the age of the superspeedway took over, with Charlotte, Atlanta, Rockingham, Michigan, Texas, Talladega and Ontario playing host to the men and machines.

The future is already upon the sport and the realization of stock car racing's potential has yet to come because no one knows where it is.

The big iron continues to thunder by and it doesn't matter if it's Daytona or Greenville-Pickens. The High Wind will hit you smack in the face and you'll be caught in its draft.

Philip Holmer
NASCAR Director of Public Relations

Daytona International Speedway
April 1971

ACKNOWLEDGMENTS

I would like to express my appreciation to all those who helped me with THE HIGH WIND. Houston A. Lawing, now a Speedways Corporation executive, gave me my first ticket to the first race run at Daytona, and has helped me in countless ways ever since. T. Taylor Warren, NASCAR's Chief Photographer, is responsible for the vast bulk of the photographs with a NASCAR credit line. He took the photograph used on the jacket, and got himself arrested in the process by an overzealous deputy sheriff who was convinced that a sane man wouldn't risk his life as Taylor was doing, just to take a photograph. Mr. Warren's rather incredible memory for names and dates was very valuable as we selected pictures from dusty files. Jim Foster and Joe Whitlock, of the Speedways Corporation, were more than helpful. Similarly, Lin Kuchler, Russ Moyer and Bill France, Jr. went far out of their way to help me. Bill Tuthill gave me much of his valuable time. The lion's share of the credit, however, belongs to Phil Holmer, NASCAR Public Relations Director, who worked long and hard on this book. It just wouldn't have been possible without him.

Neither would it have been possible without the support of William H. G. "Big Bill" France. Like everything else connected with stock car racing, Bill France's blessing is half the battle. It is a measure of the man, I think, that while he opened NASCAR's files to me, and let it be known that the book has his and NASCAR's support, there was never a suggestion that I submit the manuscript to him for any sort of correction or editing.

NASCAR people — drivers, mechanics, owners, officials and fans — are good people to work with. I hope I have done a decent job of telling their story.

W. E. Butterworth
Fairhope, Alabama
April, 1971

CONTENTS

Foreword   v

Acknowledgments   vii

Introduction   x

1 Beginning on the Beach   1

2 The Rules of the Game   13

3 Growing Pains   26

4 The Cars   50

5 The Drivers   71

6 The Tracks   99

7 The Hall of Fame   121

NASCAR 1971 Book of Rules   127

INTRODUCTION

No one knows where, or when, but everyone is agreed that the first automobile race happened the first time two cars met on a street and their drivers gave in to the urge to see which one was faster.

The first formal, organized race took place in France, in June of 1895. After 48 hours of hard driving between Paris and Bordeaux, a (French) Panhard rumbled across the finish line and telegraph operators flashed the word across Europe of the incredible average speed: *15 miles per hour!*

A car which would run more than 50 miles without a breakdown was as much of a novelty in those days as a car which could make 15 or 20 miles per hour, so the next two races (from Paris to Vienna and Paris to Berlin) were as much endurance contests as speed matches.

For most Europeans — and for that matter, Americans — the question of who won the next two races still hasn't been decided. There was a great deal of argument concerning how much time should be allowed for repairs, and whether, for example, a broken wheel was the same kind of "permissible" damage as the damage caused by running into a farmer's cow.

Outside the cities, the roads were seldom paved. When dry, they were covered with great clouds of powdery dust. When wet, they were rutted swamps. Wet or dry, they were generally lined (and sometimes blocked) with people, horses, dogs, farm carts and bicyclists as early race fans crowded around to get their first look at the marvelous horseless carriage.

An American, James Gordon Bennett, became fascinated with automobile racing on three levels. Personally, he thought it was fine sport. As a newspaper publisher, he recognized the great interest of the public in races and racers and decided it would soon become big news, like prizefighting and war. Finally, as an American, he felt that Americans would soon start building the best cars in the world and that the way to prove this — to take the reputation away from the European manufacturers — was to have races that proved his point.

He laid down rules for racing, stipulating that the Gordon Bennett Trophy would be awarded to the fastest car in a race to be held annually, starting in 1900. Each country could enter as many as three cars, but every part on each car had to be made within that country.

There were six Gordon Bennett Trophy races (1900-06), but after that the French, then the largest manufacturers of automobiles in the world, decided that the prestige of France and its auto manufacturers (who felt they should invariably have won, but hadn't) was being handicapped by the three-car limit and withdrew from competition. They organized their own racing system, the Grand Prix system. While Grand Prix wasn't rigged to give France an advantage, neither was it designed to keep France's star under a basket.

Grand Prix racing, with timeouts for both World Wars,

William K. Vanderbilt at the wheel of his Mercedes racer.

continues to this day. The French Grand Prix racing almost immediately effectively killed the Gordon Bennett Trophy races, but starting in 1904, an annual 300-mile road race for the Vanderbilt Cup was held in America. There was enough prestige and money in these races to merit European cars and drivers being shipped over by boat from Europe for them. The Vanderbilt races were held until 1917, when they were called off because we had entered World War I. Most of the Vanderbilt Cup races were held on Long Island.

Farther down South, starting in 1908, American promoters organized the American Grand Prize Interna-

Henry Ford, who hired the first professional race driver, Barney Oldfield, (at the steering lever) and their race car.

tional Road Race at Savannah, Georgia. The American Grand Prize lasted until 1916, when it failed partly because of finances and partly because of the war in Europe: An American car (a Mercer, in 1914) had won only once and, with war in Europe, no Europeans were able to come to the United States.

In 1909, in Indiana, the first race was held at the Indianapolis Speedway, then a 2.5-mile, macadam-paved circular track. Two years later, over a track paved in brick, the first Indianapolis 500-mile race was run. First winner at the "Brickyard" was a Marmon, driven by Ray Harroun at an average speed of 74.59 miles.

The Indianapolis Speedway, with timeouts for World Wars, is still very much in business, and is still called the "Brickyard" although the track has long since been resurfaced.

Between World Wars I and II, there was racing all over the country but, except for Indianapolis, it could not be considered a national sport. Races were held at county fairs, at some tracks (the Langhorne Speedway, in Pennsylvania, for example) using "Indianapolis" cars, three-quarter cars, "midgets" and even "micro-midgets," not much larger than their drivers. With the exception of Indianapolis and Langhorne and a very few other tracks, however, it wasn't a sport, really, but rather a spectacle, very often just one more attraction in the carnival atmosphere of a state fair. Everybody was a champion, because there was no real racing organization except the American Automobile Association (AAA) and the United States Automobile Club; and anyone was just free to call himself a champion of any category, nor was any prize awarded by either the USAC or the AAA.

When racing resumed after World War II, there wasn't much of a change: Race drivers were often little more than vagabonds, running cars which were unsafe, on tracks which were unsafe, for very little money. The racing promoters were sometimes carnival operators, who regarded the drivers as just another variety of strong man or two-headed freak, to be cheated wherever and however possible.

The annual 500-mile race at the Indianapolis Speedway, which offered great drivers driving superb cars for large purses, was the exception rather than the rule.

In the South, there was another kind of racing, born in the transport of moonshine liquor in the Carolina hills. Needing cars faster than those owned by revenue agents, moonshine runners built them by feel, trial, and error. They were good cars and their drivers were highly skilled. It was natural that they should start to race each other in "stock cars," in competition, for money.

It was a good idea, but there were many problems common to other kinds of auto racing: Dishonest promoters who frequently took off with gate receipts; unsafe tracks and unsafe cars; a lack, in other words, of honest organization and control.

NASCAR, the National Association for Stock Car Auto Racing, was born to fill the void. In the beginning — and today — NASCAR consisted in the main of the ideas and knowledge and guts of a man named William Henry Getty France. This is the story of NASCAR and of Bill France, because the two are inseparable.

William H.G. France.

CHAPTER ONE
Beginning on the Beach

Without much doubt, William Henry Getty France, Sr. — "Big Bill" France — is Daytona Beach, Florida's most famous — and very possibly its richest — citizen. He arrived in what was to become the high speed racing capital of the world in the fall of 1934, en route to Miami, in a battered car carrying himself, his wife, his son Billy and $25.00 in cash. In addition, there was a nest egg of $75.00 in a Washington D.C. bank.

France lets it be known that he was born in Horse Pasture, Virginia, on September 26, 1909. Other biographies list Washington, D.C. as his birthplace, and France is probably the most successful graduate of Washington's Central High School, where he put his six feet four inches to good use on the basketball team.

France's father was a bank employee and France worked part time in his high school years as a clerk in Washington's Commercial National Bank. While finance certainly fascinated him, he soon displayed a far greater interest in his own money than in other people's and after graduation took a job as a battery and electrical system repairman in a Washington gas station. It wasn't

1

Bill France at the wheel of an early stock car. *Courtesy Wm.H.G. France*

as prestigious as being a budding banker, but it paid better.

He moved up from the gas station to a Ford dealership, where he became a skilled front end repairman, and from the Ford agency to a Buick agency. Like other kids of his age, with a few dollars in his pocket, access to the family car and dreams of glory in his eyes, France spent some time and money competing in minor stock car races in the Washington-Baltimore area.

A student nurse, Anne Bledsoe, from a North Carolina mountain hamlet called Nathan's Creek, first saw Bill France, Buick front-end man and part-time race driver, at a dance given by her school, the Children's Hospital School of Nursing. The attraction was mutual. They were married June 23, 1931, in Washington.

It was the time of the great economic depression of the 30s, and they decided that Washington didn't offer as much for the future as Florida might. They loaded their few possessions, baby Billy and Big Bill's mechanic's tools into an old car and trailer and set out for Miami. Nurses and mechanics might not make any more — and possibly even less — in Florida, but at least they'd be out of expensive Washington.

In October 1934, they arrived in Daytona, where they stayed, because the car collapsed. It must have been a total collapse, for France was a skilled mechanic. There is no record that the Chamber of Commerce greeted the new arrivals with a brass band, a speech of welcome, or even a free glass of orange juice. In any event, France took whatever work he could find while he looked the town over.

He decided that operating a service station would put a roof over the family's head, food on the table and still give him time to look around for something else to do. On the strength of the reputation he had established in Washington, he opened a service station with no capital and added to the gas pump profits with front end and electrical work.

Bill France in front of his Daytona Beach service station, 1936.
Courtesy Wm. H.G. France

Sir Malcolm Campbell.
NASCAR

Daytona Beach has an auto racing history dating back to 1903. The tightly packed sands of its beach (500 feet wide at low tide; 23 miles long) were for half a century considered to provide the fastest course in the country. In 1935, Sir Malcolm Campbell drove his "Bluebird" down the sands at 276.82 miles per hour.

The next year, the city of Daytona Beach promoted a "stock car" race, for regular street automobiles, over the same course. It's been said that the city was less interested in the fastest car than in the tinkle of cash registers the spectators would cause.

Gas station proprietor W. H.G. France, who had prospered enough to own a 1935 Ford, entered in the race and finished fifth. He didn't make any money, and neither did the "event," but France saw that whoever had thought up the stock car racing idea was on the right track to make a lot of money. He wasn't discouraged when the promoters of the 1937 race lost money, too.

In 1938, the promoter of the stock car race across

Daytona's beach was Bill France. He professes to remember little about the race, except that he made "a little profit."

He made a little more profit the next year and a little more the year after that, and then the war came and racing was shut down for the duration. France spent the war years as a defense worker, building submarine chasers at the Daytona Beach Boat Works.

In 1946, he was back being promoter of the Daytona Beach races. The races had been mildly successful before the war; they were now unqualified successes. People had money to spend and there seemed to be a greater fascination in stock car racing than there was in any other kind.

France branched out a little, promoting races in North and South Carolina and in Georgia. The drivers of the cars and many of the Georgia-Carolina spectators themselves had learned about fast cars (the same cars) and skillful driving up close, in the unofficial — and perhaps even more thrilling — races between the forces of John Law and John Barleycorn. But they were, France saw, willing to pay for the privilege of watching fast cars go around a track.

It was not all duck soup. The euphemism France uses for describing racing in those days is "haphazard." The late race driver Joe Weatherly put it more bluntly. He said that racing, pre-NASCAR, saw the public cheated, the drivers cheated and the whole sport earning a bad name and becoming involved with a bad element.

A promoter, for example, would sell tickets to a race by announcing that thirty-five drivers would compete. When the fans showed up, they would find that the drivers numbered fifteen or so. Some drivers had been

5

lured to other tracks by the promise of more money and some drivers simply decided that they didn't think it was worth their while to race that day.

Some promoters saw nothing wrong in slipping money to a driver supposed to race at one track, to get him to race at another. Others felt that there was absolutely nothing wrong in telling the public the prize was a great deal of money, when in fact it was very little money, or none at all.

The drivers, on the other hand, felt no deep sense of loyalty to any track or promoter. It was every man for himself, no holds barred and get yours while the getting's good. Promoters were known to pocket the entire proceeds from ticket sales and depart with it for parts unknown. If they were not missed until after the race, only the drivers were mad. If they were missed before the race and the drivers felt no urge to risk their necks with no prize money waiting for them, both fans and drivers were mad.

On top of this, there was simply no organization. There was no set of rules for a race, no specifications for a car, no established standards for driver qualifications, no guarantee that a promoter would pay the prize money he announced, no guarantee that a driver who agreed to race would actually show up, and, important at least to the drivers, no adequate system of insurance.

Joe Weatherly, one of the all-time racing greats, who was not known for handing out undeserved bouquets, put it this way: "France was the answer to a lot of drivers' prayers."

Among promoter France's other interests was one in the Ebony Bar, atop the Streamline Hotel (now LeRoy Jenkins' Palace Inn). On December 14, 1947, France

6

Joe Weatherly.   *NASCAR*   Bill Tuthill.

convened there a meeting of men who he felt met two
qualifications: They were important in the sprouting
business of stock car racing and they were honorable
men, interested in the long term future of stock car
racing, rather than in the fast, quick buck. Some others
showed up, men whose interest in stock car racing was a
sort of offshoot of their basic interest in fast cars as a
means to get away from the revenuers, and some others
whose reputations as race hustlers were well deserved.
Since there was no organization, they couldn't be barred.

The respectable race fans and promoters and drivers
who showed up included Bill Tuthill, who owned a
motorcycle agency in New Rochelle, New York, and who
promoted stock car and other races in his area. Louis
"Red" Vogt, an Atlanta garage owner who had built cars
for Bill France to race, was there and so were people like
Joe Littlejohn, Alvin Hawkins, Tom Gallan, Bob Rich-
ards, Bill Streeter, Marshall Teague, Buddy Shuman,
Bob Osiecki, Sam Packard and Harvey Tattersall.

7

Tuthill and France were the leaders. Tuthill served as chairman of the meeting, which could not really be said to hold great promise of success. The hustlers could see no real reason to get involved with something which sounded as if it were going to be terribly legitimate and might even give the drivers and the fans a fair shake for their money.

Some of the more honest promoters felt that nothing would really come of the idea, because racing struck them as being unmanageable except in specific cases and localities. They seriously questioned whether, if they did form an organization and come up with some rules, they could get anyone who didn't feel like it to obey the rules. Racers, fans, drivers and promoters alike had a well-deserved reputation for individuality, coupled with a monumental lack of respect for constituted authority.

But they all agreed, for their own reasons, to the premise that if they, that handful of men gathered in a bar on a hotel roof, didn't do anything, then it was certain that no one else would. The feeling seemed to be that even if the idea didn't stand much chance of working, it should be explored.

They turned to first things first. They set up a Technical Committee, "to set up rules for displacement" under Chairman Ed Samples, of Atlanta. Next, a Competition Committee, under Chairman Fred Dagavar, of New York, was named and charged with establishing "rules governing a race program and to set out rules how a race should be run."

Fred Dagavar nominated Bill France to be "President of the Governing Body," and a vote was taken. The motion was carried. Then Dagavar said that they'd better list all those present and make the list part of the official records, so that, for example, if someone ever wrote a book about NASCAR, he would know who was there at the beginning:

Bill France	Buddy Shuman	Bill Tuthill
Red Vogt	Ed Bruce	Bob Osiecki
Freddy Horton	Marshall Teague	Joe Ross
Sam Packard	Chick Dinitale	Fred Dagavar
Red Byron	Frank Mundy	Tommy Garback
Eddie Bland	Bill Streeter	Bill Perry
Harvey Tattersall, Jr.		Bob Richards

Red Byron moved that the new organization be called the *National Stock Car Racing Association (NSCRA)*. But there was already a racing organization in Georgia calling itself that, so Bill France moved that everybody write down what he thought the organization should be called and pick the name that way. France couldn't get anyone to second his motion.

Red Vogt then suggested *The National Association for Stock Car Automobile Racing (NASCAR)*. NASCAR and Red Byron's NSCRA were put to a vote. NSCRA won, seven to four and then the discussion started again: There *already was* an NSCRA in Georgia. Ed Bruce moved that the balloting for NSCRA be ignored, that the new organization be incorporated in Florida and that it be called National Association *of* Stock Car Auto Racing. Jack Peters seconded the motion, and NASCAR was born.

France then said he felt that an organization like NASCAR should, as in professional baseball and football, have a man of knowledge, wide reputation, ability and unquestioned integrity as "Commissioner." France suggested that they appoint E.G. "Cannonball" Baker, the

9

Indianapolis racing great, as "High Commissioner." Eddie Bland seconded the motion and it was carried.

There was some further discussion on a point system to determine the champion drivers, zones for racing, a benevolent fund, insurance and so on, and then some final elections of officers: Bill Tuthill was named Secretary; Eddie Bland, Vice-President; and Marshall Teague, Treasurer.

France was well aware that a certain lack of legality was a major problem in racing. The solution to that was to get a lawyer involved. The problem was the lack of money.

Attorney Louis Ossinsky, who practiced law on Main Street in Daytona, was a man admired by France for a number of reasons. He was a former star tackle for the University of Georgia. He was a racing fan. And he actually paid cash money for his gasoline at France's service station.

Ossinsky (on a work-now, pay-later basis) put together a corporation based on what France and Tuthill (mostly France) thought it should be and what the law, and common sense, permitted.

NASCAR, which came into official corporate being on February 21, 1948, was set up as a private Florida corporation, much as though the three stockholders (France, Tuthill and attorney Ossinsky) had decided to go into any other business, from growing oranges to making movies.

The business of NASCAR was to "sanction" stock car automobile races. The word "sanction" comes to English from Latin via the French language. In Latin, *sanctionem* meant to "render sacred." In French *sancire* means to "render inviolable." The second definition is: "The

10

Attorney Louis Ossinsky,
shortly before his death on
January 13, 1971.
NASCAR

provision of awards for obedience, along with punish-
ments for disobedience, to a law."

Sanction was a well-chosen word.

It was decided right at the beginning that NASCAR
would have no other business; that, specifically, it would
never own racetracks, never race cars, or hire drivers.

This was an important decision by the majority stockholder in NASCAR, Big Bill France, because he firmly
believed that there was a good deal of money to be made
in race promotion and in speedway operation. (Either by
renting a track or owning one.)

So from the beginning, too, France decided that he
was fully capable of wearing two hats: One of the nine
races sanctioned in the first year (1948) of NASCAR by
NASCAR President Bill France, was the Daytona Beach
Road & Beach Race, promoted by William Henry Getty
France.

11

GENERAL RULES

All tracks must be inspected by NASCAR or its representative before a sanction will be granted.

NASCAR or its representative reserves the right to reject any entry for failure to comply with any rules or regulations.

In all NASCAR sanctioned races, when checkered flag is given to winning car, the race is officially over and all cars will stop on that lap. Finishing positions will be paid according to distance run, whether car is still running or not.

No race shall be run over 5 laps on the caution flag without stopping the race. This is to be at the discretion of the steward.

In the event of a protest, $500.00 must be deposited with NASCAR representative by driver making his protest within 10 minutes after completion of event. Protest fee will be forfeited and applied to hospital fund if judges and scorers rule against protest. The decision of judges and scorers is final. Appeal of any protest can be made in writing to the NASCAR Board of Governors for consideration at the annual convention but appeal will not change above rules on day of race and all positions will be paid according to the decision rendered.

These rules are subject to change on recommendations of the Committee.

Notice of any rule changes or additions will be sent to NASCAR members from national headquarters.

... Retain These Rules For Future Reference ...

1948
RULES AND SPECIFICATIONS

COMMISSIONER
E. G. "Cannonball" Baker — Indianapolis, Indiana

BOARD OF GOVERNORS
President
Bill France — Daytona Beach, Florida
Promoters
Eddie Bland — Jacksonville, Florida
Bill Tuthill — Hartford, Connecticut
Owners
Bob Osiecki — Atlanta, Georgia
Fred Dagavar — New York City
Drivers
Red Byron — Atlanta, Georgia
Buddy Shuman — Charlotte, N. C.
Mechanics
Marshall Teague — Daytona Beach, Fla.
Red Vogt — Atlanta, Georgia
Roadster Advisory Committee
Ed Bruce — Berea, Ohio
Jack Peters — Berea, Ohio

Technical Committee:	Competition Committee:
Ed Samples, Chairman	Fred Dagavar, Chairman
Red Vogt	Joe Littlejohn
Bob Osiecki	Tom Galan
Buddy Shuman	Bill France
Marshall Teague	Jimmy Cox
Fred Horton	Bill Tuthill
Chick Di Natale	Ed Bruce
Bill Streeter	Harvey Tattersall
Eddie Bland	Sammy Packard
Alvin Hawkins	Joe Epton

NATIONAL HEADQUARTERS
29 Goodall Ave. Daytona Beach, Fla.

1948 RULES and SPECIFICATIONS

1. Cars eligible—1937 models and up through 1948. '37 and '38 models must have 4-wheel hydraulic brakes.

2. Later models must be run in the same model chassis.

3. Foreign manufactured cars will not be permitted.

4. If car is a convertible type, it must be run with top up and in proper place and must be equiped with safety hoops mounted to frame.

5. All cars must have full stock fenders, running boards and body if so equipped when new, and not abbreviated in any way other than reinforcement.

6. Stock bumpers and mufflers must be removed.

7. Crash bars may be used no wider than frame, protruding no farther than 12 inches from body.

8. All doors must be welded, bolted or strapped shut. Doors blocked will not be permitted.

9. Fuel and oil capacities may be increased in any safe manner. Any extra or bigger tanks must be concealed inside car or under hood.

10. Wheel base, length and width must be stock.

11. All cars must have safety glass. All head light and tail light glass must be removed.

12. All cars must have full windshield in place and used as windshield. No glass or material other than safety glass may be used.

13. Cars must be equipped with rear view mirror.

14. All cars must be subject to safety inspection by Technical Committee at any time.

15. All cars must have 4-wheel hydraulic brakes or any brake manufactured after 1947.

16. Piston displacement in any car is limited to 300 cu. in. except where motor is used in same body and chassis it was designed and catalogued for. Under 300 cu. in. motors may be interchanged in same manufacturer's line.

1948 RULES and SPECIFICATIONS

17. Any block can be oversize. The only truck blocks permitted to be used in any Stock Car will be 100 H. P. Ford Blocks which are fundamentally same as passenger car. These may only be used in models up to 1947 Fords. (Stock interchangeable passenger car blocks must be used in all cars through 1947.)

18. Cars may be run with or without fan or generator.

19. Any fly wheel may be used.

20. Any part may be reinforced.

21. Any interchangeable wheel or tire size may be used.

22. Any rear end arrangement may be used.

23. Any radiator may be used providing stock hood will close and latch properly. Hoods must have safety straps. All cars must have hoods on and must be stock hood for same model car.

24. Any type battery ignition may be used, excluding magnetos.

25. Any type of manufactured spark plug may be used.

26. Any model manufactured flat type cylinder heads may be used. Cylinder heads may be machined to increase compression.

27. Heads allowed with overhead valves only when coming as standard or optional equipment from factory.

28. Any valve springs may be used.

29. Multiple carburetion will be permitted. Any type carburetion may be used.

30. Superchargers allowed only when optional on stock equipment by manufacturer.

31. Water pump impellers may be cut down.

32. Altered cam shafts will be permitted.

33. Altered crank shafts may be used.

34. All drivers must be strapped in and must wear safety helmets. Belt must be bolted to frame at two points and must be aviation latch type quick release belt.

35. Regulation crash helmets must be used.

The Committee recommends for the 1949 season that 1937 Models be dropped from competition

NASCAR

CHAPTER TWO
The Rules of the Game

NASCAR established its first National Headquarters at 29 Goodall Avenue, Daytona Beach, and promptly published "1948 Rules and Specifications" for NASCAR racing.

It was not a very impressive document, physically. Printed on one sheet of heavy paper, it measured about eight inches square. It was folded in the middle, so there were four pages. The front page featured, for the first time, the now very familiar NASCAR insigne, two checkered flags and two stylized winged cars and the legend, "National Association for Stock Car Auto Racing, Inc."

There were immediately wisecracks that the insigne was very appropriate, showing, as it did, two high speed cars on an obvious collision course.

The front page listed, below the insigne, the names of the Commissioner ("High" Commissioner having been dropped somewhere along the line), "Cannonball" Baker, the Board of Governors, and of the Technical and Competition Committees. The two inside pages, with plenty of white space left over, listed the 35 rules thought necessary for stock car auto racing. Some of the rules seem very innocent.

Number 3, for example, read: "Foreign manufactured cars will not be permitted," and Number 13 read: "Cars must be equipped with rear view mirror."

The back page stated that tracks had to be inspected by NASCAR before a sanction would be granted; that NASCAR reserved the right to reject any entry for failure to comply with rules; that races would be over when the checkered flag was given to the winning car, and all others would stop on that lap; that no race, at the discretion of the steward, would be run more than five laps with the caution flag out; called for a $500 deposit to NASCAR by a driver making a protest, the money to be forfeited to the hospital fund if the protest wasn't upheld; stated that the decisions of judges and scorers were final; announced that the rules were subject to change on recommendation of the Committee and admonished readers to retain the rules for future reference.

Twenty-two years later, in 1971, NASCAR rules were published in a 98-page closely printed booklet and sold for $1.50.

The first NASCAR-sanctioned race was held before the incorporation papers had actually gone through the courts. On February 15, 1948, on the road-and-beach course at Daytona Beach, Red Byron won first place. Marshall Teague came in second, and Bob Flock placed third. The Corporation became official on February 21, and on February 24, at Jacksonville, Florida, the first post-incorporation race was held. Fonty Flock took first place, Bob Flock second and Red Byron third.

Fifty-two races were sanctioned by NASCAR during 1948. Seven in Greensboro, N.C.; six in North Wilkes-

Red Byron, who won the very first NASCAR sanctioned race.
NASCAR

Marshall Teague.   *NASCAR*

Bob Flock.   *Jack Cansler*
Photo from NASCAR

Fonty Flock.   *NASCAR*

boro, N.C.; five in Lexington, N.C. There were four NASCAR-sanctioned races in Charlotte, N.C., and in Macon, Georgia. Other races were held at such places as Dover, New Jersey, Occoneechee, N.C., Langhorne, Penna., and Atlanta, Georgia.

Fonty Flock won 15 of the 52 races, placed second in nine, and fourth in three. Right on his heels was Red Byron, who took the checked flag eleven times, placed second five times, and third four times. Curtis Turner

15

placed first seven times; second, twice; and third, five times.

On May 30, 1948, at Jacksonville, Florida, a name that was to be one of the most famous ever in NASCAR racing — or for that matter, in auto racing without qualification — appeared: Glenn "Fireball" Roberts. He ran second, after Paul A. Pappy and ahead of Lamar Woodall. Not quite a month later, on June 20, Cotton Owens placed second at Greensboro, N.C. Buck Baker, another all-time great, placed third twice in the first year of NASCAR racing, at Martinsville, Virginia, on July 4, and at Greensboro, N.C., on July 25.

NASCAR was off and running.

In 1949, NASCAR sanctioned 87 stock car races, on 25 speedways from Fort Lauderdale, Florida, to Buffalo, New York. From their new headquarters at 800 Main Street in Daytona Beach, France proudly announced annual figures that today sound like the returns from one race.

Competing drivers took home $181,289 in prize money. (In 1970, NASCAR paid out $5,389,350 in prize money.) In addition there was $6,775 in championship point money for the season. (The North Carolina Motor Speedway at Rockingham, for one example, paid out $6,875 in championship point money for just one race, the 1969 Fifth Annual American 500, in addition to $82,825 prize money.)

The most important development of 1949, however, was the introduction of Grand National racing. NASCAR President Bill France sanctioned the first Grand National race, 150 miles at the Charlotte, N.C. Speedway, on June 19. The promoter was William Henry Getty France. France also promoted Grand National races at North

(l-r) Dorothy Beech, Bill France and Ed Otto sign the 1950 NASCAR Point Fund checks.

Wilkesboro and Hillsboro, N.C., Daytona Beach, Florida, Martinsville, Va., and Langhorne, Penna. Promoter Ed Otto staged Grand National races at Pittsburgh, Penna., and at Hamburg, N.Y. France and Otto paid out something around $40,000 in prize money for all eight races in the Grand National category. Today, $40,000 is not considered big money at all for *one* Grand National race (for example at the *first* race held at the Bryan, Texas, Speedway, on December 7, 1969, the purse was $71,485).

More than 500 NASCAR-licensed drivers competed in various categories of racing all over the country, on all sorts of tracks, without a fatal injury. France and others in NASCAR insisted this was because the tracks and the cars met NASCAR specifications for safety, and there was little argument about that, but all was not entirely peaceful.

Five drivers were charged with conduct detrimental to

17

racing at Charlotte and after a trial, four of them were suspended. Jimmy Thompson was found innocent and reinstated, and Marshall Teague was reinstated later in the year.

The other three drivers remained suspended for the rest of the season, and the word got out that NASCAR's bite was real. One driver, whose car was found wanting by NASCAR technical inspectors at Charlotte, took the matter to the courts. He charged, in the federal court at Greensboro, that France and NASCAR, separately and together, were running a monopoly, and that, since General Motors was forbidden to have a monopoly, so should France and NASCAR be forbidden. After two days of hearings (and held breath by France and NAS-CAR) the suit was dismissed. NASCAR had passed its first and only major legal test to its claim to be the governing body for stock car automobile racing.

The names of Fonty Flock, Curtis Turner and Red Byron continued to head the list of frequent winners and record setters, but there was also a lady in the running: Sarah Christian, of Atlanta, was named Champion Lady Driver of 1949. She ran sixth (in a field of 45) at Langhorne; fifth (against 22 men) at Pittsburgh and fourth (against 44 men) at Syracuse.

Twenty-two thousand people were on hand to watch the first Grand National race. Glenn Dunaway, of Charlotte, took the checkered flag, but when his car was inspected after the race by NASCAR technical inspectors, it was disqualified, and Jim Roper, who had run second, was named the winner.

Bill Tuthill, at the end of the 1949 season, owned 40% of the NASCAR stock. It's generally believed that France held another 40% and lawyer Ossinsky the remaining

20%, although, as a closed (non-public) corporation, the figures do not have to be made public. They never have been.

Tuthill felt very strongly that Ed Otto, who had been promoting auto and motorcycle racing in large cities (Buffalo, Jersey City, Rochester, etc.) in the Northeast should be made a part of NASCAR. France was perfectly happy to have Otto join, but he felt that Otto should be required to buy in. Otto couldn't quite see it that way. Tuthill figured that without Otto, NASCAR (which, despite the glowing figures published and France's high hopes, had sanctioned only 85 races in 1949) might well fold, and that his 40% of NASCAR might turn out to be 40% of nothing.

He offered Otto half of his 40% interest in NASCAR (20% of the outstanding stock) for nothing, if Otto would affiliate with NASCAR. Otto accepted, and now that he had an interest, used his influence to get other race promoters to participate, including Robert Barkheimer, of California, which spread NASCAR influence to the West Coast.

France kept his block of stock intact.

The headquarters — the office — was moved to 42 South Peninsula Drive in Daytona Beach after the stock maneuvers. The first order of business there was insurance for drivers and for NASCAR racing officials while supervising races.

There wasn't exactly a long line of insurance men frantically bidding for the business. Insuring race drivers, and their associates, was then considered about on a par with insuring lion tamers, soldiers-of-fortune and stunt pilots. Policies could be obtained, in some companies, but the premiums demanded were astronomical.

France found one man who would listen to him, a Providence, Rhode Island, insurance agent named John Naughton. France managed to convince Naughton of two things, first that under NASCAR, rigid safety standards for track, car and driver would keep claims to a minimum. He admitted that there would be accidents, but pointed out that auto racing wasn't the only hazardous occupation in the world. Secondly, France managed to convince Naughton — and the actuaries of the companies Naughton represented — that NASCAR insurance was going to be big business.

To get the insurance, NASCAR had to guarantee a minimum premium of $30,000, based on a $100 premium per race. In other words, they had to sanction 300 races, and collect $100 from the proceeds of each race for insurance alone, or make up the difference from the none-too-full NASCAR treasury.

NASCAR — which is to say France, for he was now without any question the majority stockholder in NASCAR — felt that both for ethical reasons and business reasons, NASCAR had to provide for drivers and officials (who included, for example, the men who would rush out to a flaming car with a fire extinguisher) the mental security that would come with the knowledge that if they were hurt, they would immediately receive the best medical attention money could buy, and at NASCAR's expense.

Tuthill and Ossinsky agreed with him. They signed a contract with Naughton stipulating a minimum premium payment of $30,000, at a rate of $100 per race. Then they set out to find 300 races which NASCAR could honestly sanction, more than three times as many for the coming year as they had been able to sanction in the past.

They made it with room to spare, and with absolutely no compromise of NASCAR standards. During 1950, there were 395 sanctioned events, and more than 2,000 dues-paying members of NASCAR.

The first "superspeedway" made its appearance during the 1950 racing season. At Darlington, S.C. the first track designed specifically for stock car racing had been built. It was a paved 1.250-mile track, and on it the promoters announced they were going to run, on Labor Day, the First Annual Southern 500-Mile Race.

Darlington was obviously going to be big time racing, just what NASCAR needed to really get off the ground. But on the other hand, if it wasn't run by the letter of NASCAR rules, it could do NASCAR as much damage as good. France refused to issue a sanction for the race until he was completely convinced that the race would be run as publicized, and that the prize money announced was more than a hopeful statement on the part of the promoters. Finally, a little more than a month before the race was to be run on Labor Day, the Darlington promoters met the final NASCAR requirement. They deposited a certified check for $25,000 to NASCAR's credit in a Darlington bank; the prize money was now a sure thing, and France issued a NASCAR sanction.

Fastest qualifier was Wally Campbell, of Camden, N.J. Driving a new Oldsmobile 88, Campbell drove 10 miles in 7 minutes, 16.89 seconds for the best time of 82.35 miles per hour. Despite his time, and the pole position it earned, Campbell didn't finish the race, and for his trouble, took home a total of $100.00.

The winner, Johnny Mantz, driving a 1950 Plymouth, did somewhat better. It took him six hours, 38 minutes, and 40.26 seconds to go the 500 miles, for an average

Johnny Mantz, winning the first "NASCAR Superspeedway" race at Darlington, 1950.

speed of 76.26 miles per hour. He took home $10,510.

Second place went to Fireball Roberts, and it's interesting to note that the official records had started to call him "Fireball" rather than "Glenn." He was driving a 1950 Olds. Red Byron, driving a 1950 Cadillac, placed third and won $2,000. Fourth place went to Bill Rexford, in another 1950 Olds. Chuck Mahoney placed fifth in a 1950 Mercury, and Lee Petty ran sixth in a 1949 Plymouth.

Twenty-nine Oldsmobiles were entered. There were also 10 Lincolns, 9 Plymouths, 7 Fords and 7 Mercurys, 3 Studebakers, 3 Hudsons, 2 Buicks, 2 Cadillacs, 2 Nashes, 1 Kaiser and 1 Pontiac. The fact that it was really a national race, rather than a Southern race advertising itself as "National" just to sell tickets, was pointed out by the home states of the drivers: There were drivers from Virginia, both Carolinas, Georgia and Alabama, the South, which was to be expected. But there were also drivers from California — the winner, Johnny Mantz —

Minnesota, New York and New Jersey, Oregon, Ohio, Indiana, Missouri and Pennsylvania.

Grand National racing, under the auspices of the National Association for Stock Car Auto Racing, can really be said to have become both "grand" and "national" at the First Southern 500 at Darlington, on Labor Day, 1950.

Darlington immediately became the standard of NASCAR racing, as Indianapolis' "Brickyard" was and is the standard for its own specialized brand of racing. The criteria was not only speed, (although Darlington was without question the fastest track in NASCAR) but the length of the course (three years after it opened, in 1953, Darlington was extended to 1.375 miles from 1.250), and the quality of the competitors, which meant ever better cars and ever higher speeds.

In 1950, for example, Johnny Mantz took the Southern 500 in a 1950 Plymouth with an average speed of 76.26 miles per hour. In the 1953 Southern 500, the first on the 1.375-mile track, the winning speed, with Buck Baker in a 1953 Oldsmobile, was up to 92.78 miles per hour. In 1957, Speedy Thompson, driving a 1957 Chevrolet, was the first to break the "Century Mark" averaging 100.100 miles per hour for the 500 miles. The next year, Glenn "Fireball" Roberts won it in another '57 Chevy, with the average speed up to 102.590 mph. In 1959, Jim Reed, driving a '59 Chevy, upped the winning speed almost ten miles, with a 500-mile average of 111.836.

As important as the ever faster speeds was the ever greater income at the gate. Bill France, as NASCAR racing grew in prestige, never veered from his idea that the better the track, the faster the race, and the higher the income from the ticket booths.

23

Glenn "Fireball" Roberts.

The tunnel to the infield at Daytona under construction. Bill France in middle.

In 1959, the second, and soon to be most famous, of the superspeedways was opened at Daytona Beach. This was the longest (2.5 miles) stock car track ever built, and it was built with an eye to the future. The turns were so steeply banked that the road graders and paving machinery had to be held in place by cables as the track was built.

The two main races of 1959 at Daytona confirmed France's judgment. Lee Petty, at the wheel of a 1959 Oldsmobile, averaged 135.521 to win the first Daytona 500. Fireball Roberts drove a 1959 Pontiac at an average speed of 140.581 to take the checkered flag at the first Firecracker 400 meet on the new track. Ticket sales proved France's theory about fast races selling tickets.

In 1960, the Atlanta International Raceway, 1.5 miles, opened for racing, and saw Bobby Burns run a 1960 Pontiac 500 miles at an average speed of 108.624. Fireball Roberts ran his 1960 Pontiac at an average speed

24

of 112.653 to take the first Dixie 300. The next year, the Dixie became a 500-mile race, and David Pearson won it in a 1961 Pontiac, turning an average of 125.384 mph.

The same year, another superspeedway, the Charlotte (N.C.) Motor Speedway, opened for business, and saw Joe Lee Johnson wheel a 1960 Chevrolet over the 1.5-mile track at an average speed of 107.752 mph for a 600-mile distance. Later in 1961 Speedy Thompson ran a 1960 Ford 500 miles at an average speed of 112.760 to win the National 500 at Charlotte.

In 1965, the North Carolina Motor Speedway (at an even mile, the shortest of the big time tracks) opened for business to see Curtis Turner turn 101.943 in a 1965 Ford to take the American 500.

In 1969, three superspeedways opened their doors to the racing public. At Texas International Speedway Bobby Isaac averaged 144.277 mph in a 1969 Dodge to take the first Texas 500 over the two-mile loop; and at the Michigan International Speedway at Irish Hills, near Detroit, Cale Yarborough wheeled a 1969 Mercury at 139.254 mph to win the first Motor State 500, over the other new 2.0-mile loop.

The Alabama International Motor Speedway was advertised as the longest (2.6 miles) track in NASCAR racing, and "probably" the fastest. The "probably" vanished when Richard Brickhouse drove his 1969 Dodge for 500 miles at 153.778 to win the opening Talladega 500. That was the fastest race ever run, and Brickhouse was admittedly not the most promising competitor. The Professional Drivers Association, most of the top contenders, headed by Richard Petty, got in a squabble with Bill France just before race time and didn't run.

25

CHAPTER THREE
Growing Pains

NASCAR's growth was remarkable and impressive, but it was not without its battles. The mental imagery that comes to mind is of Bill France, wrench in hand, taking on, all alone like Sir Galahad, the Dragons named Ford and Chrysler, even though the industrial giants were backed up by reinforcements consisting of tire and accessory manufacturers, promoters, and even small guerrilla bands of drivers who were convinced they were being wronged.

And, like Sir Galahad, because his heart was pure and he had the strength of ten, winning hands down on all occasions.

The major automobile manufacturers quickly came to realize that one of their cars taking the checkered flag with any kind of regularity, or even frequency, was going to make the cash registers start jingling in showrooms across the nation.

General Motors rather piously announced that it wanted nothing for its customers but safety and convenience, and was not, therefore, about to subsidize automobile racing with its emphasis on speed and power.

26

While the left hand more than likely knew what the right hand was doing when Pontiac was the hot car in NASCAR racing, whatever financial and technical support was provided Pontiac drivers theoretically was without the official blessing of General Motors.

Chrysler and Ford, however, were honest enough to admit that they found NASCAR racing a wholly satisfactory means by which to attract the buying public. The race to the finish line was also a race for the customer's checkbook, and they set out to win it by means mostly fair.

It would be impossible to detail all of the incidents of near Machiavellian intrigue and all out warfare between the auto giants and NASCAR, which is, again, to say Bill France, but some idea can be obtained with a brief recapitulation of the marching, retreating, and assaults and capitulations of the war years 1964-69.

On October 16, 1964, NASCAR let it be leaked to the press that "drastic rule changes" could be expected when the 1965 NASCAR Rules were released later that month. During the 1964 season, Chrysler Corporation cars had been powered with a newly developed engine featuring a hemispherically shaped combustion chamber, immediately dubbed "the hemi." With the hemi engine, Chrysler Corporation cars, (Dodges and Plymouths) had run away with most of the races in which they ran, beginning in January.

France, who until recently had been calling for more and more speed, was beginning to have second thoughts. There had been several accidents in European Grand Prix racing, some of which had wiped out spectators, and all of which tended to give racing a bad name.

France had begun to call for "speed, but not at the

27

expense of safety." No one was especially surprised, therefore, when the NASCAR Rules for 1965, released to the profession and public on October 20, reflected France's known concern that speeds were getting too fast, mainly because of the Chrysler hemi engine. The hemi engine was banned for 1965. NASCAR also ruled that for the four superspeedways, (Daytona, Atlanta, Darlington and Charlotte) cars would have to have a minimum wheelbase of 119 inches. NASCAR also specified a maximum displacement of 427 cubic inches for engines, and stipulated that engines must be of "production design only." That eliminated hemi engines and overhead cam engines, since neither was being made available to the public, or was, in fact being produced except for the racetrack. Roller cams and roller tappets were expressly forbidden. Cars with at least 116-inch wheelbases would be permitted to run on the shorter Grand National tracks, but the engine restrictions would apply there as well.

The first casualty was the 1965 Dodge. The car Dodge had planned to run as its entry in the prestige sweepstakes was the 1965 Coronet 500, wheelbase 117 inches. Anticipating France's hemi engine decision, Dodge was producing a 426-cubic inch displacement engine within NASCAR specifications., i.e., a wedge-shaped, rather than hemispherically shaped, combustion chamber.

About this time the Mercury Division of the Ford Motor Company simply withdrew from the 1965 competition, feeling that they weren't getting their money's worth.

There was a good deal of speculation that France, threatened not only with the loss of Chrysler-supported cars in NASCAR racing, but with the chilling prospect of

Lee and Richard Petty. Those aren't love beads — Richard is promoting Florida lemons.
NASCAR

slower sales at the ticket booths because of Chrysler's departure, might change his mind or compromise.

On December 3, 1964, he ended the speculation. "The 1965 specifications are now at the printer's," France announced. "There are no changes from the announcement concerning engines and wheelbase of October 20." At the same time, France announced that the prize money at Speed Weeks at Daytona would exceed $138,765. That pot of gold, he apparently believed, would attract all the racers the track could handle.

Rumors began to spread that Lee Petty was installing a 426-wedge engine in the 1964 Plymouth in which Richard Petty would run at Riverside. Soon that rumor died. Richard Petty was sitting out the 1965 NASCAR season, and running his Plymouth elsewhere. He competed in the USAC Sanctioned Yankee 300 at Indianapolis in April of 1965, but was forced out by mechanical trouble with the car that France said, on May 15, was "a big engine in a light, short car that doesn't

29

meet our rules. Anytime that Petty, or any other driver, gets a car that meets our rules, he's more than welcome."

On May 21, France made another announcement to the press. "Chrysler," he said, "is perfectly welcome to return to NASCAR racing and can, just as soon as it manufactures a Plymouth Fury with a hemi engine on the production line." At the same time, apparently in the belief that what people don't know for sure keeps them interested, France denied knowledge of a report that Chrysler planned to have cars running in the Firecracker 400 at Daytona on the Fourth of July.

Within a month, it was official: A NASCAR spokesman said, on June 20, that Chrysler's hemi engine would be permitted in Grand National racing, on tracks over one mile (the superspeedways) so long as it was mounted in either a 1965 Plymouth Fury or a 1965 Dodge Polaris, which met the 119-inch wheelbase criteria.

Four days later, Chrysler Corporation's Chief Engineer R.M. Rodger politely but pointedly spurned NASCAR's overture: "Factory-attended Dodges and Plymouths," Rodger announced, "will not attend the Firecracker 400 (Daytona), the Southern 500 (Darlington) or the National 400 (Charlotte)."

Face was saved on both sides. Chrysler wasn't giving in to France, and NASCAR wasn't giving in to Chrysler. The second half of Rodger's announcement put Chrysler back in racing: "The rules permit the return of 1964-65 Dodge Coronets and Plymouth Belvederes to NASCAR tracks of under one mile. We see no reason why they (i.e., Chrysler-backed drivers) should not enter these NASCAR events when their schedules permit."

Ford ran away with the 1965 superspeedway races. Marvin Panch took the Atlanta 500 and the Dixie 500 at

Marvin "Pancho" Panch.   Fred Lorenzen.   A.J. Foyt.

Atlanta, driving a 1965 Ford. Another 1965 Ford, driven by Fred Lorenzen, took the World 600 and the National 500 at Charlotte, and the Daytona 500 as well. Ned Jarrett drove a 1965 Ford to win the Southern 500 at Darlington, and the Rebel 400 at Darlington went to Junior Johnson in another 1965 Ford. A.J. Foyt won the Firecracker 400 in a 1965 Ford, and to tie things up quite neatly, Curtis Turner drove a 1965 Ford to have the checkered flag waved at him at the American 500 at North Carolina Motor Speedway.

Ford was understandably pleased with itself, and not at all bashful in telling the American public that, in addition to a clean sweep of the superspeedways, it had won all but seven of the 55 Grand National races in which it had run.

For the 1966 season, Chrysler, running the now legal hemi engine, would be, France thought, rather a leavening influence. The hemi would give the Fords a real run

31

for big money, and racing would be at least relatively peaceful again.

Ford, however, having listened to the cheerful tinkling of cash registers in Ford showrooms, was determined to stay out in front in 1966 as well. The first Henry Ford had learned years before of public sympathy for the underdog when he'd made use of it quite successfully to sell the Model T. Chrysler had let it be known that they felt something like the underdog, being forbidden to run their hemi engine, and planned to straighten things out in 1966 when the hemi would be legal.

There had been much talk about engines — oh, had there been talk about engines! — including some talk that Ford might possibly run an overhead cam engine in 1966, to maintain its lead when Chrysler started running the hemi. France apparently had made the final statement on that subject: "Overhead cams engines will never be allowed in NASCAR stock car competition."

France had spoken, and it seemed to be as positive a statement of policy as, say, one by the late Charles de Gaulle. The matter obviously was resolved once and for all.

On December 14, 1965, Donald N. Frey, then general manager of the Ford Division of the Ford Motor Company, was the main speaker at the Ford Performance Awards banquet in Dearborn, Michigan. Bill France, as befitting his status as NASCAR president, was seated at the head table with other Very Important People, when Mr. Frey got down to the meat of his speech:

"Full size Ford Galaxies with a 427-cubic inch single overhead cam engine will be Ford Division's engine for stock car competition for the 1966 season."

There was sort of a hushed silence, and then Frey went on: "We have used the single overhead cam engine extensively in drag racing, and feel it will be best suited for our stock car competition." Then, "We will operate on NASCAR tracks in much the same way as we did in the 1965 season when we won all but seven of the 55 races."

NASCAR rules at that time regarding engines were not especially precise. They called for the use of only "production" engines, but production was not defined very clearly, except to say they should be in the $1000 price range, and that the bona fides of "volume" production should be determined by a NASCAR-named committee of at least two persons who would make spot checks of assembly lines when that was considered necessary, to see that a "production" engine was indeed in production.

Ford had been running a double overhead cam engine at Indianapolis, and educated guesses as to the cost of that engine ran as high as $30,000 per copy.

Mr. France had no comment to make to the racing press on the evening of the Ford announcement.

The next day, December 15, Ronnie Householder, Chrysler Corporation's chief of racing, said the obvious thing: "The ball has been thrown to Bill France. Now let's see if he drops it."

The same day, France was quoted as saying, "One of the things we have done in Detroit is watch Chrysler's hemi engine in mass production." That confirmed that Chrysler's hot engine would be running in the 1966 season.

France returned to Daytona Beach from Detroit and huddled with United States Auto Club Director Henry Banks. In a joint statement on December 17, France and Banks, or NASCAR and USAC, said that the Ford single overhead cam engine would be barred from their sanctioned races because it was experimental, not in production, and worth more than the $1000 limit set for engine costs.

The same day, in Detroit, Leo C. Beebe, director of Ford Public Relations, just as soon as the France decision had been announced, had his counterstatement ready:

"We believe the Ford plans to race in 1966 with a single overhead cam engine were completely consistent with current NASCAR rules." In case anyone had missed this bit of information, Mr. Beebe continued, "After winning 48 of the 55 Grand National Championship races, naturally we would have preferred to defend our laurels against the best the competition has to offer." Then he got to the meat of Ford's position: "Obviously, with the season's start just a month away, it will not be possible for us to prepare factory-sponsored vehicles for such races as Riverside and Daytona."

In other words, Ford was taking its ball and going home.

The next day, December 18, the drivers were heard from. Junior Johnson, Curtis Turner, Ned Jarrett and Fred Lorenzen announced that since Ford was quitting NASCAR racing, so were they.

"I've been driving for Ford for five years," said Lorenzen, "and I'll do what it does. If they don't build any cars, I'll be swimming all summer."

Ned Jarrett, the 1965 Grand National Champion, whose purses had totaled more than $70,000, said that he thought Ford had "ground to stand on. I don't blame the company."

The independent drivers were on France's side: Tom Pistone, of Charlotte, said that he had "dropped several

Junior Johnson.

Curtis Turner.

thousand dollars last season because I didn't have the money to compete with the (Ford) factory. I think me and Tiny Lund and other independents will be able to compete with conventional Ford engines against the Chrysler hemi."

The word had spread by the next day, that Chrysler was going to have as many as 20 Plymouths and Dodges ready for Speed Weeks at Daytona. If Ford wanted to quit, why that was a pity. But on the other hand, with 20 Dodges and Plymouths all with hemi engines starting at Daytona, Chrysler's advertising people were already drafting newspaper ads along the lines of "It was Chrysler Corporation all the way at Daytona."

That day, both France's and Ford's public relations director Beebe stated their positions again, more clearly: Beebe announced officially that Ford would not run at either Riverside or Daytona. France said that he'd asked Ford if they could provide 50 of their engines for sale to all comers; Ford said they could not, and that, said

35

France, proved his point that the overhead cam engine did not qualify as a production engine and was thus illegal.

The press now entered the act. In his syndicated column of December 20, 1965, Joe Whitlock told his readers not to be surprised if all NASCAR super-speedway racing in the future was done in Volkswagens, which, as we all know, don't change very much and thus pose no problems for NASCAR. He aired the often heard comment that racing was getting too commercial, and that soon no one would be allowed on the track without the blessing of Dun and Bradstreet. But he supported France:

"France apparently feels that stock car racing is now big enough to make its rules and invite anyone to play that wants to abide by them. No changes, no politicking. Nothing. All black and white. Let's hope it stays that way."

(It should be noted parenthetically that Joe Whitlock is now a NASCAR press relations official.)

The next day, December 20, John Holman, president of Holman-Moody, the shop which set up the Ford racing cars, announced that Ford would make an announcement within days whether or not it would field factory-backed cars. This was a crack in the rigid position of "If we can't race with our single cam, we won't race, period," previously very strongly implied from Detroit.

Two days later, Paul Preuss of Ford solemnly gathered the racing press before him to announce, "Rumors and reports that Ford will not compete in the American 500 race at the North Carolina Motor Speedway (Rockingham) are erroneous."

By the day after Christmas it was all over. Ford had

Ralph Moody. John Holman.

caved in all the way. Not only would they race with the "old" engine, but they would race at Riverside, the opening race of the new season. The statement, it is interesting to note, was issued from Daytona Beach, not Detroit.

For his part, Bill France was congenial. "We have been assured," he said in a formal statement, "that the single overhead cam engine will be produced in sufficient quantity by the end of 1966 so that it will comply with existing rules. The new engine could be sanctioned 90 days from the time it complies with the uniform rules."

It was an important victory for France and NASCAR and for the fans. If he had caved in under the tremendous pressure and made "an exception" for Ford, it certainly would have left little for Chrysler to do but come up with an engine to compete. That would have started a spiral between them. With the enormous technological skill and limitless money of the two giants

Jim Hurtubise and his Petty Plymouth.

NASCAR

turned free to develop powerful and sophisticated engines, within a year, perhaps less, NASCAR cars would have been powered with engines bearing absolutely no resemblance to those available to the general public, and NASCAR racing would have become a battle of advertising budgets, rather than a test of mechanical and driving skill.

It was a bitter pill for Ford to swallow, and it didn't taste any better as the 1966 season took its course. At Atlanta, a 1966 Plymouth driven by Jim Hurtubise took the Atlanta 500, and Richard Petty took the Dixie 500 in another '66 Plymouth. Marvin Panch took the World 600 at Charlotte in a 1965 Plymouth and LeeRoy Yarbrough took the National 500 in a 1966 Dodge. Driving a 1966 Plymouth, Richard Petty also took the Rebel 400 at Darlington, plus the Daytona 500 at an incredible average speed of 160.627, a time that was to stand for at least five years. Sam McQuagg won the Firecracker 400 at Daytona in a 1966 Dodge, and Paul Goldsmith drove a 1966 Plymouth to win the Carolina 500 at North Carolina Motor Speedway.

38

Ford did have some wins: Fred Lorenzen took the American 500 at North Carolina in a 1966 Ford, and Darel Dieringer, at the wheel of a 1966 Mercury, won the Southern 500 at Darlington; but Ford couldn't say, after the 1966 season, that they'd won all but seven of the races they'd entered. Neither could they, or for that matter Chrysler or anyone else, make their plans behind locked boardroom doors for upcoming seasons without paying very close attention to the NASCAR Rule Book.

France had proved, once and for all, that he was making the rules, and if you wanted to play in his ball game, you played by his rules. On their part, Ford and Chrysler seemed to realize that it was to their interest to stay in racing, and subject their products to the testing fire of open competition.

Or, so some people said, for at least a couple of weeks.

Mario Andretti and Fred Lorenzen placed first and second in the 1967 Daytona 500, driving 1967 Fords. The

Mario Andretti in the Winner's Circle after the 1967 Daytona 500.

engine they were running was the 1966 engine, improved by the incorporation of a new manifold and new exhaust system. Jacques Passino, a Ford vice president in charge of special (racing) vehicles, announced that there was a 5% horsepower increase in the engines equipped with the new manifold and exhaust.

"Foul!" cried Chrysler, shortly after Daytona.

Ronnie Householder, Chrysler's performance chief, on March 24, 1967, charged that the new exhaust and manifold made the Ford engine illegal. But it wasn't in the nature of an official complaint to NASCAR because, since the previous summer, Chrysler was officially not sponsoring cars for NASCAR racing. The key word in that sentence is "officially." What really had happened was that Chrysler executives had apparently cut that part of the budget set aside for racing activities.

From Cotton Owens' Dodge shop at Spartanburg, and from Lee Petty's Plymouth shop had come howls of outrage that their financial support from Chrysler had been cut just about in half. Worse than that, Petty and Owens were complaining publicly that Chrysler was charging them up to twice as much for Chrysler racing parts as Ford was charging their "affiliated" garages for the same kind of Ford racing parts.

It appeared to many people that Chrysler's complaint about the new manifold and exhaust systems on the Ford engines was a combination of sour grapes and a possible excuse for them to quit racing entirely.

Householder called a press conference and defined his complaint: "Ford's new engine belongs in the same category as their single overhead cam engine," he said, making reference to the engine that France had barred from racing as "non-production." "The rules," House-

Cotton Owens. *NASCAR*

NASCAR Vice President Lin Kuchler. *NASCAR*

holder said, rather primly, "plainly state that the engine must be of standard production. Not just for a preferred few. All we want," he concluded, "is enforcement of the rule book. Isn't that what a rule book is for?"

Cotton Owens chimed in the same day and spilled the beans about whether or not Chrysler was lending only moral support to Chrysler products. "We're still on the Chrysler payroll," Owens said, "and we will have to do what the bossman says."

Lee Petty seemed annoyed at everybody. "We were in racing before Chrysler got in," he said, "and we will be racing after they get out. I don't know if we'll be affected by this controversy or not."

Lin Kuchler, NASCAR vice president, lost no time in announcing NASCAR's position: "The Ford engine is still the same basic 427-cubic engine used all along. The new manifold system and exhaust system is an improve-

41

ment, that's all. And it's cheaper. Ford has simply replaced old parts with new ones, and the engine needs no approval."

Richard Petty let it be known publicly that he could not "afford to run the 100-mile dirt track races without some help," and his father pointedly chimed in with the statement that the Petty team would continue to race, because "racing is our livelihood."

This might possibly have been construed by someone in the Chrysler corporate hierarchy as a thinly veiled threat that the Pettys would swap brands.

All of this was on March 24.

On March 25, it became known that some Chrysler entries in the Atlanta 500 were being withdrawn, and Chrysler modified its unofficial complaint to include the cylinder heads on the Ford engines, which it said were not standard production items and were not available generally.

"We tried to buy them, and couldn't," a Chrysler spokesman announced. He didn't say what he had planned to do with the Ford heads if he had been successful.

The drivers of Chrysler products now tried a little pressure of their own. They applied to enter the Atlanta 500 Race "contingent upon" (rather odd language for race drivers) NASCAR enforcement of Rules 1-C1 and 14A of the NASCAR Rule Book. These were the rules that covered engine eligibility and minimum production and defined what a standard production cylinder head should be.

NASCAR's response to this was that NASCAR didn't accept contingency-loaded applications; you either applied to race or you didn't apply to race.

On Sunday, March 26, Chrysler flexed the muscle in its velvet glove. Chrysler, it was announced, would "withhold support" (which, theoretically, it wasn't providing anyway) to any driver who raced in the Atlanta 500.

An anonymous comment went around the track: "What Chrysler is sore about is that Cotton won't cheat as much as they think he should." Cotton Owens played by the rule book. He thought that trying to slip something past a NASCAR technical inspector was dishonest, and he simply wouldn't do it.

Chrysler had another plaintive, heart-tugging comment to make that Sunday: "We wanted to give racing back to the sport," a Chrysler spokesman said with a straight face, "but found out it wasn't wanted."

Richard Petty that day laconically announced he had filed an application to race his Plymouth in the Atlanta 500, and, "as things stand now, intend to race."

R.M. Rodger of Chrysler issued still another statement: "Chrysler Corporation strongly supports the position taken by Dodge and Plymouth stock car drivers this week involving their protest over NASCAR's refusal to enforce the 1967 rules."

Lin Kuchler of NASCAR came right back at him: "The Chrysler action comes as no surprise to us. They said last year they planned to greatly curtail stock car racing activities. We have had no formal protest from Chrysler about the Ford parts."

Since Chrysler was officially not fielding cars, they couldn't file an official protest. Presumably, Mr. Kuchler knew this.

On Tuesday, March 28, with the Atlanta 500 scheduled for the following Sunday, Chrysler caved in. There was a sort of face-saving agreement between Chrysler and Bill France that NASCAR would "review" the situation further on the Monday after the race, but Chrysler-built cars would run.

There is a temptation to consider these fracases as what Shakespeare described as a lot of "sound and fury, signifying nothing," but actually that wouldn't be a solid assessment. What really happened was that Bill France, because there was no one else, decided what was the right position to take, and stuck with that position against the sort of pressure only major automobile manufacturers can exert.

The name of that game could fairly be called, "Bet Your Sport." For France, whose money was tied up in Daytona and other superspeedways, it also meant betting his fortune. A racetrack is an expensive hobby if you can't get paying customers to fill its seats. He stood in danger of going broke when he stood by what he believed was right for the future of auto racing, and for the benefit of the fans. In an era when important men are often concerned primarily with number one, France's guts and integrity are admirable.

France has had several skirmishes, and one major battle with the drivers. He built, near Birmingham, Alabama, at Talladega, the Alabama International Speedway. It was the longest (2.6 miles) and most expensive (over $3,000,000) of the superspeedways, designed to be the fastest (over 200 mph) track of them all.

The drivers, banding together under Richard Petty in the Professional Drivers Association, had presented to France a number of demands, including an increased percentage of the gate receipts, a more generous pension plan and some other things, and timed their demands to coincide with the opening of Talladega.

Their apparent reasoning was that France was at that moment most vulnerable. He certainly would want to have Talladega open under the most auspicious of circumstances, and not with a nasty bruhaha involving the big name drivers, with the big name drivers possibly pulling out of the race after the fans had paid good money in the belief that they would run.

In other words, they figured he would have to give in. They finally had Big Bill where they wanted him.

France again held firm. The drivers, he said, knew the rules of the game. If they wanted to play by the rules, they were welcome. If they wanted to pull out of the race, the responsibility for disappointing the fans was theirs, not his.

They thought he was bluffing, and they called his bluff. But France went through with his promise to pay the prize money, a total of $91,950.00 to whoever ran. Richard Brickhouse chose to run. Brickhouse, when the 1969 season was over, was in 25th place, with 1660 Grand National Points, and a purse total of $45,312. (David Pearson, in first place with 4160 points, took home $183,700 for 1969, for purposes of comparison.) $24,500 of Brickhouse's total winnings came from Talladega, which he took in a 1969 Dodge at an average speed of 153.778 mph.

Richard Brickhouse.

NASCAR

The First Family of NASCAR Racing: William C. "Bill Junior"; "Big Bill" and Anne France, and James, (fresh from the 82nd Airborne Division in Vietnam).

It was a fine race, the fastest of any Grand National race for 1969, and the fans couldn't complain that they didn't get their money's worth. But France thought that since they had bought their tickets thinking they were going to see Petty and the other big names drive, and they hadn't, the thing for him to do was to give them a racing rain check. Tickets for the next Talladega 500, he announced, would be given free to anyone who had paid to see the opening race and had the stubs to prove it. The gesture cost France well over half a million dollars.

At this writing, Bill France is having no trouble with the Professional Drivers Association, or with any automobile manufacturer. If there is trouble, say, starting tomorrow, and there well may be, the smart money is being laid on Bill France to come out on top, smiling, and pretty sure of himself.

For an organization as large as NASCAR, the staff is relatively small. Number Two man is William C. "Bill, Junior" France, who is a vice president of NASCAR (and executive VP of the International Speedway Corporation). A Navy veteran, France has two children and lives in Daytona Beach. Literally having grown up in NASCAR, Bill, Jr. has been called upon to do everything from flagging races to standing in for his father at the most important of meetings. James France, the youngest son, is fresh from duty with the 82nd Airborne in Vietnam. He's learning the business, too, starting like his brother at the bottom.

Lin Kuchler, NASCAR vice president, is a long time motorcycle racing executive and driver. He came to NASCAR from a job as executive secretary of the American Motorcycle Association.

Russ Moyer is the executive manager of NASCAR. A former newspaperman from Pennsylvania, Moyer is in charge of NASCAR administration of everything from tickets to racing licenses.

Chief Scorer and Timer for NASCAR is Joe Epton. He's held the job since NASCAR was founded. At his first race, he had one assistant. At last year's Daytona 500, he had more than 120 people keeping track of the score and times.

John Bruner, Sr., who first worked with France and NASCAR during the beach races in 1949, is chief steward of the Grand National Racing Division, and assistant director of competition.

Bill Gazaway, a former Marine, aircraft engine builder and competition garage owner, is chief technical inspector.

There are three NASCAR Regions: Eastern, Western and Pacific Northwest. Former race driver Bob Sall, with NASCAR from the beginning, is Eastern field manager. Bob Barkheimer, who founded the California Stock Car

47

Russ Moyer.   Joe Epton.   John Bruner, Sr.

Bill Gazaway.   Bob Sall.   Bob Barkheimer

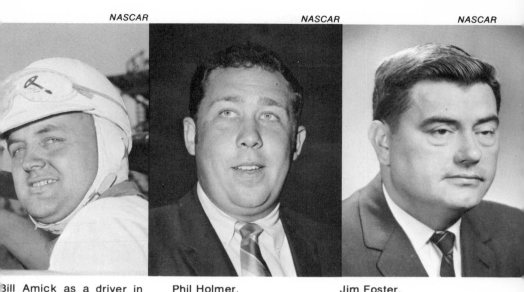

Bill Amick as a driver in　　Phil Holmer.　　　　　　Jim Foster.
1955.

Racing Association in 1949, and brought the organization
into NASCAR in 1954, is Western regional director. Bill
Amick, a driver who ranked 16th in the 1956 Grand
National Point Standings is manager for the Pacific
Northwest.

The youngest member of the NASCAR hierarchy is 28-
year-old Phil Holmer, the public relations director. A
three-sport athlete at Culver Military Academy, Holmer
holds degrees in journalism and political science from
Bradley University.

Holmer replaced long-time director of public relations
Jim Foster, who is now in charge of publicity for the
Daytona and Talladega International Speedways. The
two jobs, of course, are, when NASCAR is running,
closely interconnected.

49

CHAPTER FOUR

The Cars

The term "stock car" originally meant just that. Bill France, for example, got started in racing at the wheel of the family Buick. But that term no longer precisely applies. A two-door sedan fresh off a showroom floor is obviously not going to be able to turn onto a track at Talladega and run for 500 miles at speeds in excess of 175 miles per hour. The tires wouldn't stand that pace, nor would the engine or transmission. And if something happened, and a truly "stock" car happened to crash into a barrier, doing 165 mph, the driver would be killed instantly, as the body and chassis collapsed around him.

Just about as soon as NASCAR began to operate, they began to stipulate precisely what changes to "stock" cars had to be made in the interests of safety, and with equal precision, what changes could, and could not, be made in the car itself to make it run faster. These have evolved into many pages of closely printed rules and regulations, and may be found in Appendix One.

Preparing a "stock" car for racing has evolved into one of the world's most highly skilled professions. All drivers readily admit that without a well "set-up" car, they

The Master's touch: Everett "Cotton" Owens, characteristic
toothpick in mouth, with Dodge hemi engine.

couldn't compete, much less win. A well set-up car requires more than a skilled mechanic to replace parts and tune an engine to a fine degree. A NASCAR Grand National racing mechanic has to be, first, a superb mechanic, a past master at that trade, and second, he has to have a profound knowledge of racing — both the techniques a good driver must use to win, and an understanding of the difference in tracks and weather conditions and other factors which will affect car performance.

The best mechanic, it follows logically, would be a mechanic with racing experience of his own. It's not surprising, therefore, that one of the very best NASCAR mechanics is a Spartanburg, S.C. garage owner who began in NASCAR racing as a driver. Everett Owens, universally known as "Cotton," started racing in 1946, and was soon known as the "King of the Modifieds."

In 1950, he won 54 major races on the Modified Circuit, 24 of them consecutively. In 1959, driving a Grand National 1958 Pontiac, he set a world's record for the fastest qualifying time ever run at the first Daytona 500. The next year, he earned the pole position with a lap-time of 149.6 miles per hour. In the first race at the Atlanta International Speedway — the Dixie 300 — he ran seconds behind Fireball Roberts to take second place. When Bobby Johns took the Atlanta 500 later in the year, he was at the wheel of a Pontiac set up by Cotton Owens.

When Cotton Owens retired as a driver in 1962, he had taken the checkered flag for first place in nine Grand National races. The next year, he started setting up Dodges for Grand National competition, and training the drivers to run them. His first driver was David Pearson, who happened to be a Spartanburg neighbor. Pearson was Grand National Champion in 1968. Owens had also trained "Chargin' Charlie" Glotzbach, who came in second at the 1969 Daytona 500 by 1/100 second. Buddy Baker, of Charlotte, N.C., has been driving front-running Owens Dodges, and what follows is the story of how Cotton Owens set up his cars:

Cotton Owens prepared two cars for the 1970 racing season, both Dodge Charger "Daytonas."

At one time, the first step in building a Grand National racer was to tear apart what the dealer had delivered. Recently, however, it has been possible to order from the factory a stripped-down version of the street model. This not only eliminates much of the waste of discarding parts that can't be used, but also saves the builders' time.

The first step was to remove what ornaments and extras remained on the "stripped" cars. All the chrome went, the emblems, the headlights and the interior. Next, every part which would be placed under a greater strain than the passenger-car designers had intended was removed and replaced by a substantially stronger part.

Substantially stronger parts than stock are now available from the manufacturer. Until 1964, car builders either had to reinforce what came with the car or build what was needed. Some of the "racing" parts are further strengthened by a builder like Owens when he feels that it is necessary.

A Grand National car will have a top speed of

Cotton Owens and Buddy Baker in serious conversation. The Owens-Baker Daytona which first broke the 200-mph lap record is behind them.

somewhere near 225 miles per hour. It will enter a turn going somewhere between 180-190 miles per hour. The law of centrifugal force begins to make itself felt at these speeds and the builder must contend with the laws of aerodynamics as well. The fastest jet fighter becomes airborne at speeds beneath 180 mph.

The idea is to lower the center of gravity of the car; to see that the weight distribution between the front and rear wheels is the most advantageous; and to insure that the springs, shocks, swaybars, tie-rods, control arms and spindles are substantial enough to take the enormous stress which will be imposed on them.

The strengthening process began with the chassis. All the welded joints were re-welded, and more welding was applied wherever it seemed that doing so would increase the chassis' rigidity. Steel tubing was welded to the front frame rails, both to strengthen and stiffen the rails, and to provide a place to which additional shock absorbers could be attached. The upper control arm brackets were braced, and the rear of the frame had more steel tubing welded to it, which in turn was connected to the roll bars, providing even more strength and rigidity.

The roll bars, of course, have the important function of providing protection for the driver, as well as strengthening the chassis. NASCAR specifications stipulate steel tubing of .090" wall thickness and not less than 1.75 inches in outside diameter, connected at top and bottom on both sides at seat height. Each door, below the window opening, was provided with a fence-like arrangement of this sturdy steel pipe, connected to the cross bars just below the roof, and with the cross members inside the passenger compartment. It is aptly described as the "cage."

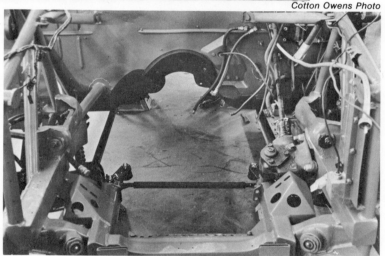

The Daytona's engine compartment after modifications, awaiting the engine. It has a heavy-duty Pitman arm and idler arm, a modified "K" member to make room for the large dry-sump oil pan, a modified opening to clear the exhaust headers, and a fresh air cowling (top center) to duct air.

For the front suspension, standard tie-rods, upper and lower control arms and shock absorbers were removed. Heavy duty tie-rods and control arms were installed in their place, fixed to reinforced mounting points. Two extra-strength, extra-length shock absorbers per wheel

55

The right front suspension. Note dual shock absorber installation, special racing brake lining, and heavy duty upper control arm and tie-rod.

Cotton Owens Photo

were installed. The dual installation provided extra strength and reliability, and the extra length provided greater travel without "bottoming" for the wheel. For stability, an extra heavy-duty sway bar was installed, and for strength and reliability, hubs and spindles of special quality steel were built and installed.

Braking at speeds far greater than any encountered on any superhighway requires special brakes. The standard passenger car brake drums were removed, and replaced with the heavy-duty brake drums furnished on police cars. Woven standard brake lining tends to harden and cause "fading" when subjected to extreme heat, so it was removed and replaced with Cerematalix lining. This special lining actually increases braking efficiency as temperature rises. On the other hand, it isn't quite as

56

effective as standard lining unless it is quite hot.

Braking is a tricky area. The brakes have to be hot enough to insure functioning of the Cerematalix lining. But they can, especially on some shorter tracks, where a good bit of braking is necessary, get too hot. The answer to this is to duct air to blow on the brakes, to keep them at the proper temperature for most efficient operation.

Deciding how much air is necessary is one of the finer points of the mechanic's art that separates Cotton Owens, and the half dozen other top racing mechanics, from the others, for it isn't simply a mechanical decision, but one based on their assessment of the track, the temperatures likely to be encountered, and the kind of a race which will be run. Consequently it is never the same decision.

After making a professional assessment of each race at each track as it would apply to the rear suspension, Cotton Owens provided different springs for each track on which his cars would run. Passenger cars on the roads turn right as often as they turn left; Grand National tracks all turn only to the left, so provision is made to transfer weight to the left wheels to counteract the centrifugal tendency to shift weight to the right on turns.

All standard spring shackles and hangers were removed from the cars, and specially made, very substantial and adjustable brackets were installed in their place. By adjusting the brackets (and raising and lowering the springs) it is possible to shift weight around to suit track conditions. This adjustment is based often on long and earnest conversations between the driver after test laps, and the chief mechanic, who must envision in his mind what is needed. It is not an area with much room for mistakes in judgment.

Specifically made, adjustable spring brackets permit adjustment for all racing conditions.

Cotton Owens Photo

Cotton Owens Photo

Dual shock installation on rear end. One shock on each side is forward of rear axle, one on each side to rear. Upper ends are fastened to special bracket in trunk.

For the rear suspension, holes were cut into the metal floor of the trunk to provide room for the longer shock brackets necessary for the longer, wider, dual shock installation. At superspeedway speeds, air pressure would build up in the trunk as it rushed through the hole cut through the trunk floor to the point where it would pop open the trunk or fill the passenger compartment. Snap-on pads were installed to keep the air and dust out of the trunk.

The extra length of the shock absorbers also required a special bracket extending below the axle housing. Be-

58

cause of the centrifugal force on the left turns, the axle housing was fitted with baffles to keep all the grease from collecting on the right side, and the housing itself was vented to relieve the high pressure built up inside by the long, high-speed running.

The rear end, running at speeds three times that for which it was designed, would quickly generate heat which would burn it out without a means of cooling. Inside the car, behind the driver, a radiator was installed, with an electric fan to blow air through it. The radiator contained the grease with which the rear end was lubricated. The grease was pumped by a 12-volt electric sump pump from the rear end through the radiator, cooled by the air flowing through the radiator, and then returned to the rear end.

Each car was provided with as many as a dozen different rear end gear assemblies, to provide the most efficient operation on any given track. The use of a particular gear is again the result of lengthy conversations based on test running between the driver and the chief mechanic. The idea is to match the most efficient speed of the engine (Cotton Owens feels his Dodge engines are most efficient in the 7,200 rpm range) with a gear that will put the car out in front of the others and keep it there without blowing the engine.

Owens' Grand National Dodge Daytonas have "full floating" axles; they do not support the weight of the car. They simply transfer power from the rear end to the wheels. The weight of the car is transferred through the steel hub to the axle housing. With this arrangement, if an axle should break, the car will continue rolling. With the axle supporting the car's weight, "lock-up" occurred, often with disastrous results.

NASCAR gave its "Award of Excellence" to Goodyear for its development of the "Lifeguard" inner tire for racing. Shown here with Joseph Hawkes, Goodyear's chief tire design research engineer is a cut-away tire, showing the inner tire, which carries 80 pounds of pressure, and will permit safe stops if the outer tire blows at racing speed. *NASCAR*

Richard Petty tested the tire-in-a-tire concept himself by blowing all four tires shown here with small explosive charges while moving around Daytona at racing speed.

Goodyear

To provide a "free-floating" axle, a special adapter was pressed into the axle housing, under many tons of pressure. Then a bearing hub, carrying two tapered roller bearings, was attached to the adapter.

Racing wheels are 9.5 inches wide, and greatly strengthened for the additional stresses of racing. Tire selection involves a third expert, the man from the tire company. Firestone and Goodyear both provide racing rubber for the prestige they get when their tires are on a winning car. From a large choice of available tires, the final decision again is often reached between the driver

60

Steve Petrasek, Firestone's racing tire designer, with tire designed for dirt track racing.

Firestone

Firestone

Bill McCrary, Firestone's racing manager, poses with Firestone's largest passenger car tire (left) and a tire to be used at Darlington's "Southern 500" Grand National NASCAR race.

and the chief mechanic, who combine their knowledge to pick the best one.

The engine in the Dodge Daytonas run by Buddy Baker is a 426-cubic inch displacement "hemi" (making reference to the shape of the combustion chamber). The single carburetor has four barrels, to comply with NAS-CAR rules. The engine is rated at 575 horsepower.

NASCAR rules prohibit the souping up of an engine by increasing its displacement, or by the use of a roller cam. What is permitted, what makes Cotton Owens an acknowledged master of his trade, is called "blueprinting." It's a slang term, but one universally accepted and understood by the racing profession.

What it means is that the actual engine is compared to the blueprints for the engine. For example: The blueprints will specify that a piston should weigh so much. Owens will insure that each piston in his engine will weigh, within grains, just as much as every other piston. A set of perfectly balanced pistons will get more performance from an engine than would be possible with "nearly balanced" pistons. The difference, of course, is minute, but it's important.

The intake manifold system is described on the blueprints. NASCAR rules permit "polishing and porting" of the engine. With a master's touch, Owens will see that there is nothing in the inside of the engine which could possibly interfere with the smooth flow of the air-fuel mixture to the cylinders. The compression ratio of the engine as delivered is 10.5. Owens raised this to 12.5. The engine had a transistorized ignition system, and the distributor had dual breaker points, designed for the high revolutions which would be required. (As of April 1, 1971, no magnetic impulse ignition system is permitted.)

The problem that heat is a product of high speed revolution and that heat tears up engines was partially resolved by increasing the engine oil capacity almost threefold, to 18 quarts. The word *partially* applies because Owens engines are regarded as wholly satisfactory if they can "go the distance" of the race without blowing. Even with an 18-quart capacity, his engines are subjected to such stress that after one race they may require rebuilding. There is no chance whatever that they will last 1/20 as long as an engine in highway use.

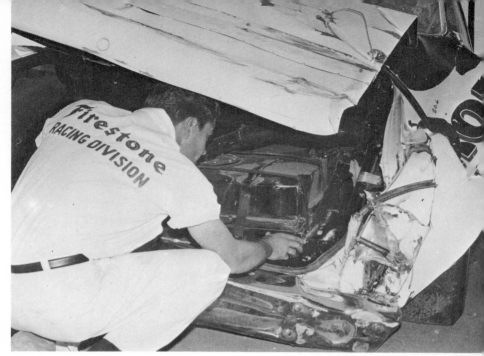

Not a drop of gasoline was lost from its fuel cell when this NASCAR Grand National car wrecked at more than 160 mph.

To remove the burned fuel-air mixture from the cylinders, a system of specially constructed, high capacity, tubular exhaust headers was installed, and these were connected to straight exhaust pipes, without mufflers, extending out the right side of the car behind the driver.

The standard, four-speed stick shift transmission is sufficiently sturdy for use in a racing car, although the standard shifting mechanism itself was replaced with a heavy duty Hurst floor shift, providing both greater strength and a quicker shift of gears.

NASCAR rules limit fuel tanks to a capacity of 22 gallons, and also require the use of a fuel cell. Harvey Firestone himself put his engineers to work on a crash basis to develop a fuel tank system which would not

The Firestone race car fuel cell. *Firestone Drawing*

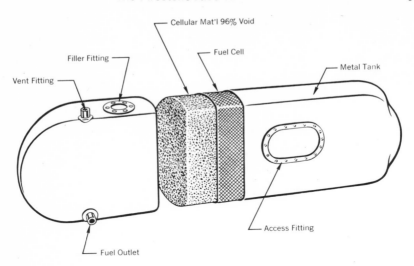

- Cellular Mat'l 96% Void
- Fuel Cell
- Filler Fitting
- Metal Tank
- Vent Fitting
- Access Fitting
- Fuel Outlet

rupture in a crash after the fatal crash which took the life of NASCAR's all time great driver, Fireball Roberts. It's generally accepted that Firestone, which makes available both complete tank-and-bladder systems, and bladders separately, loses money on each sale.

Cotton Owens made his own tank, containing the Firestone safety bladder. The tank and filler neck were installed as one unit in the dead center of the tank. The breather tube was extended through the trunk on the Daytona, and out the top and out of the top left side tail light, and covered. A rubber hose connected the filler tube in the tank to an outside filling point on the left side. NASCAR rules insist that the filling system be stock. In the case of the Dodge, this meant an outside dimension of 1.25 inches. A standard cap for the filler tube was used, but it had a short length of cable fastened to it, and to the car, to keep it from being lost either during a pit stop, or from the severe vibration encountered on the track.

The severe vibrations to be encountered on the track, as well as space considerations, required that Owens move the battery location to a position against the left front of the firewall. The battery support was reinforced, and the standard passenger car battery replaced with a very heavy duty truck battery. The reservoir for the extra crankcase oil, a welded, stainless steel tank, was mounted immediately above the new battery location.

Standard motor mounts would not stand up under the strain of either the high speed or the sudden tremendous acceleration Grand National racing requires, so they were strengthened by welding.

A heavy duty truck battery is mounted below the oil reservoir on the front left wirewall.

Cotton Owens Photo

A stripped down Dodge Daytona, after sheet metal work and engine compartment reinforcement, waiting for the 426-cubic-inch engine.

Both heat and vibration would overwhelm the standard water radiator, so a specially built racing radiator assembly providing greater strength, greater heat dissipation, and with a greater ability to resist clogging by dirt, was installed. Just in front of the radiator, a smaller radiator was installed, for crankcase oil. Oil is pumped from the crankcase to the oil radiator, where it is cooled, and then pumped to the reservoir over the battery, and finally back to the crankcase.

A good deal of effort and skill went into the passenger compartment. A bucket seat was firmly mounted to the chassis. The driver is protected by a heavy duty safety

The reinforced radiator installation, oil radiator in front, water in rear.

belt, buckling across his lap. A standard aviation type shoulder harness holds his shoulders in place. (Aviation harnesses are designed to protect in high speed impact; they can be used with only minor modifications as they come from the box). Owens installed a third safety belt, attached to the floorboard and the seat belt, which would keep the driver from sliding downward (and out of) the shoulder and seat belts in the impact of a crash. All the belts were provided with quick-disconnect fasteners.

The interior of a Cotton Owens NASCAR Grand National Dodge Daytona. Note heavy padding on steering wheel and roll bar cage.

The steering wheel was heavily padded with foam rubber and leather.

The standard instrument cluster was removed from behind the dashboard, and replaced with an array of heavy duty gauges necessary for racing. There is no need for a speedometer (which would be unreliable in any event at racing speeds), and none is provided. The most important instrument, a tachometer, was installed in the center of the cluster of gauges. There was a water temperature gauge (0-250 degrees Fahrenheit); an oil temperature gauge (100-325 degrees) and pressure gauges for oil pressure (0-100 pounds) and fuel pressure at the carburetor entrance (0-10 pounds).

The glove compartment was sealed shut, and the doors locked from the inside by the use of four welded fasteners bolted closed with 3/8-inch bolts. All of the standard upholstery was removed. Door panels and the like were replaced with sheet aluminum fastened with

Both the "Spoiler" (under nose at front) and stabilizer on truck give 200-mph plus racer stability.

Cotton Owens Photo

sheet metal screws. The lower interior was then painted black, and the upper interior (e.g., the roof) painted white.

Very little was done to alter the appearance of the exterior body, but there were significant, if unobtrusive, changes. The headlight openings were closed with cut-to-fit sheets of aluminum. At speeds in excess of 150 miles per hour, air pressure will build up under the front of the car, turning it into sort of a wing. A carefully designed aerodynamic spoiler, of 6 x 1/8-inch aluminum was fitted across the entire width of the front tread, six and a half inches off the ground, and at a 45-degree angle.

A "safety stabilizer" (actually a wing) was installed 24 inches above the rear of the trunk lid. It can be adjusted sixteen degrees, to push down on the rear of the car. Precise adjustment of the stabilizer (adjusting the downward "push") is again something reached after testing by the driver and much thought by Chief Mechanic Owens.

Air rushing into the engine compartment at racing speeds would immediately build up pressure under the hood and rip it loose from standard hood fastening devices.

Cotton Owens installed three safety pins through the hood, fastening to the metal work surrounding the engine compartment. The holes around the pins were reinforced. When the hood is closed, thick, spring-metal clips are inserted in holes in the pins. They're attached to the frame with a plastic-coated steel cable, like that on the gas cap, so they can't be lost from vibration, or dropped on the ground during a quick pit stop.

To keep the trunk lid in place, two pin installations were made there.

NASCAR rules require that Grand National cars have full, clear, standard windshields and rear windows. All side windows must be removed. As of May 1, 1971, on all tracks of any length, a NASCAR-approved nylon screen must be installed in the driver's side window. Both the windshield and the rear window require reinforcement to keep them from popping out. Owens bolted the front window in with five bolted-on clips, and installed two, tape-covered, 1/8 x 1-inch metal straps over the rear window to keep it from blowing out under pressure.

Owens estimates that it costs an absolute minimum of $18,000 to set up a standard car for NASCAR racing, and adds, "It costs a lot more than that to set up a winning car." That's not hard to understand.

CHAPTER FIVE
The Drivers

NASCAR drivers are among the most interesting — as well as the best paid — athletes in the world. While it's not really a young man's sport (people simply can't acquire Grand National or Grand American driving skills overnight), most of the drivers are in their late twenties or thirties. Fred Lorenzen and Bobby Isaac are both (as of 1971) thirty-eight. Richard Petty is thirty-five. Lorenzen began Grand National racing in 1956, however, when he was twenty-two. Bobby Isaac was twenty-seven when he ran his first Grand National race in 1961. Richard Petty was twenty-one when he began Grand National racing in 1958.

On the other side of the calendar, Wendell Scott ran his first Grand National race in 1961, when he was 40 years old. At 49, he entered 41 Grand National Races. Bill Champion began Grand National racing in 1955 at 34. At 49, he entered 38 Grand National Events.

There are some drivers who haven't made it through high school, and some (Ed Hessert and Don Tarr) who slip off a medical doctor's whites to put on a fire resistant driver's suit. Some do nothing but drive. Others, like Roy

Bill Champion.   Donald Tarr. M.D.

Mayne, have jobs that sometimes keep them from racing. As Technical Sergeant Mayne, Roy is an Air Force career man. Some are in racing for the money and nothing else, and some are in for the thrill, and then there are people like William LeRoy Tyner, a Cherokee Indian who devotes just about all his free time to the Holy Angels Nursery for crippled, deformed and retarded children in Belmont, N.C.

Most of the drivers are married, and wives (and children) are generally just out of camera range when Daddy gets kissed by Miss Whateveritis in the Winner's Circle. While some of the older drivers recall brushes with the Internal Revenue Service in the old days, most drivers today would be called "square" by many people.

72

Roy Mayne. USAF. Roy Tyner.

There isn't much drinking, and there are far fewer female race followers around NASCAR pits and garage areas than there are in Grand Prix or even Sportscar racing.

There are some drivers who pride themselves on never working up a sweat outside the track, and others who take great pride in their physical fitness. Across Volusia Avenue from Daytona is a jai alai court. Some drivers go there to watch, and some go to compete with the professionals in another of the world's toughest sports.

Almost without exception, drivers are models of courtesy, decorum and safety on the highway. Phil Holmer, the NASCAR public relations director, tells the story of an understandably anonymous Grand National driver he followed out of the parking lot at Daytona one afternoon. Holmer said he watched the driver shift naturally from first to second, and from second to high, and then keep accelerating. Soon he was touching 100 miles an hour through Daytona traffic. Just as surprisingly, he screeched to a halt at a red light, and Holmer caught up with him to inquire what the trouble was.

"No trouble," the driver reported. "Why do you ask?"

"Do you know how fast you were going?" Holmer asked. The driver's face lost all color when Phil told him, and the next day he had a governor installed on his car which keeps it under 65 miles an hour.

The drivers are proud that their sport is "clean." It has never been touched by even a suggestion of dishonesty. Part of this is because there is simply no way to figure the odds of NASCAR racing, and the gamblers have to go somewhere else to make a bet.

Drivers are rated officially on points. (See the Rule Book, Appendix One, for the method of winning points.) The NASCAR Champions for the last 22 years are:

GRAND NATIONAL

1949 - Robert (Red) Byron, Atlanta, Ga. (Oldsmobile)
1950 - Bill Rexford, Conewango Valley, N.Y. (Oldsmobile)
1951 - Herb Thomas, Sanford, N.C. (Plymouth-Hudson)
1952 - Tim Flock, Atlanta, Ga. (Hudson)
1953 - Herb Thomas, Sanford, N.C. (Hudson)
1954 - Lee Petty, Randleman, N.C. (Chrysler)
1955 - Tim Flock, Atlanta, Ga. (Chrysler)
1956 - Elzie (Buck) Baker, Spartanburg, S.C. (Chrysler-Dodge)

1957 - Elzie (Buck) Baker, Spartanburg, S.C. (Chevrolet)
1958 - Lee Petty, Randleman, N.C. (Oldsmobile)
1959 - Lee Petty, Randleman, N.C. (Oldsmobile-Plymouth)
1960 - Rex White, Spartanburg, S.C. (Chevrolet)
1961 - Ned Jarrett, Conover, N.C. (Chevrolet)
1962 - Joe Weatherly, Norfolk, Va. (Pontiac)
1963 - Joe Weatherly, Norfolk, Va. (Pontiac)
1964 - Richard Petty, Randleman, N.C. (Plymouth)
1965 - Ned Jarrett, Camden, S.C. (Ford)
1966 - David Pearson, Spartanburg, S.C. (Dodge)
1967 - Richard Petty, Randleman, N.C. (Plymouth)
1968 - David Pearson, Spartanburg, S.C. (Ford)
1969 - David Pearson, Spartanburg, S.C. (Ford)
1970 - Bobby Isaac, Catawba, N.C. (Dodge)

GRAND AMERICAN

1968 - De Wayne (Tiny) Lund, Cross, S.C. (Mercury Cougar)
1969 - Ken Rush, High Point, N.C. (Chevrolet Camaro)
1970 - Dewayne (Tiny) Lund, Cross, S.C. (Chevrolet Camaro)

LATE MODEL SPORTSMAN

1950 - Mike Klapak, Warren, Ohio
1951 - Mike Klapak, Warren, Ohio
1952 - Mike Klapak, Warren, Ohio
1953 - Johnny Roberts, Baltimore, Md.
1954 - Danny Graves, Gardena, Calif.
1955 - Billy Myers, Germanton, N.C.
1956 - Ralph Earnhardt, Kannapolis, N.C.
1957 - Ned Jarrett, Conover, N.C.

75

1958 - Ned Jarrett, Conover, N.C.
1959 - Rick Henderson, Petaluma, Calif.
1960 - Bill Wimble, Lisbon, N.Y.
1961 - Dick Nephew, Mooers Forks, N.Y.
1961 - Bill Wimble, Lisbon, N.Y. (Co-champions)
1962 - Rene Charland, Agawam, Mass.
1963 - Rene Charland, Agawam, Mass.
1964 - Rene Charland, Agawam, Mass.
1965 - Rene Charland, Agawam, Mass.
1966 - Don MacTavish, Dover, Mass.
1967 - Pete Hamilton, Dedham, Mass.
1968 - Joe Thurman, Rocky Mount, Va.
1969 - Charles (Red) Farmer, Hueytown, Ala.
1970 - Charles (Red) Farmer, Hueytown, Ala.

MODIFIED

1948 - Robert (Red) Byron, Atlanta, Ga.
1949 - Fonty Flock, Atlanta, Ga.
1950 - Charles Dyer, North Bergen, N.J.
1951 - Wally Campbell, Trenton, N.J.
1952 - Frankie Schneider, Sandbrook, N.J.
1953 - Joe Weatherly, Norfolk, Va.
1954 - Jack Choquette, West Palm Beach, Fla.
1955 - Bill Widenhouse, Midland, N.C.
1956 - Charles (Red) Farmer, Hialeah, Fla.
1957 - Ken (Bones) Marriott, Palm Harbor, Fla.
1958 - Budd Olson, Paulsboro, N.J.
1959 - Glen Guthrie, Washington, D.C.
1960 - Johnny Roberts, Baltimore, Md.
1961 - Johnny Roberts, Baltimore, Md.
1962 - Eddie Crouse, Glen Allen, Va.
1963 - Eddie Crouse, Glen Allen, Va.
1964 - Bobby Allison, Hueytown, Ala.

1965 - Bobby Allison, Hueytown, Ala.
1966 - Ernie Gahan, Dover, N.H.
1967 - Carl (Bugs) Stevens, Rehobeth, Mass.
1968 - Carl (Bugs) Stevens, Rehobeth, Mass.
1969 - Carl (Bugs) Stevens, Rehobeth, Mass.
1970 - Fred DeSarro, Hope Valley, R.I.

Drivers — especially among themselves — have another means of classifying drivers: "How much does he make?"

Twenty drivers in the NASCAR active drivers record book have made at least $100,000 each in prize money. This doesn't take into consideration any other money (point fund money, accessory manufacturers' prizes, or the like.) These are the winners: (All data is through the 1970 season).

Robert Arthur "Bobby" Allison, 34, of Hueytown, Alabama, is married and has four children. He stands five feet eleven inches tall and weighs 160 pounds. A hunter and fisherman when he's not on the track, he's also very active in religious affairs in the Birmingham area. Since he ran his first Grand National race in 1961, he's started in 201 races, won 19 of them, and placed in the top ten 113 times. He's driven a total of 40,654 miles on Grand National tracks, and his Grand National winnings total $329,826.00. He also raced in five Grand American races in 1968 and two in 1970, and brought home $3,810.00 for those efforts. He was NASCAR Modified Champion in 1964 and 1965.

Donnie Allison, Bobby's brother, two years younger, is also married with four children, and also lives in Hueytown, Alabama. Donnie has run in 69 Grand National races since 1966, and won five of them. He placed in the

Bobby Allison.
Rossi Engineering

Bobby Allison wrapped this one up in the 1969 Firecracker 400 — and walked away from it.

top ten 39 times and his Grand National purses total $238,641.00. In 1968, he ran in twelve Grand American races, and won five of them for $10,625.00 in Grand

Donnie Allison (left) talks racing tires with Goodyear's race tire expert Chuck Blanchard.

American purse money. Donnie stands 5 feet nine inches and weighs 175 pounds.

Elzie Wylie Baker, Jr., of Charlotte, N.C., is far more widely known as "Buddy." He carries 215 pounds on a six-foot-five frame. Married, and with two children, Buddy is the first man to turn a 200-mile plus lap in Grand National racing. (200.447 mph at Talladega.) He ran his first Grand National races at 19 in 1959, and has started in 290 Grand National races in his career. He's won only three of them, but he's always been near the winners. He's placed in the top five 61 times, and in the top ten 106 times. In 43,960 miles of Grand National racing, he's won $298,881.00.

Elzie Wylie Baker, Sr., is far better known as "Buck," and sometimes as "Buddy's Daddy." In 1970, at 51, he

Buddy Baker.

Buck Baker.

This father told his son to go out and drive it as fast as he could. Buddy and Buck Baker with Buddy's Chevrolet in 1958.

Courtesy Buck Baker

Buddy Baker

Buck on Beach at Daytona with his 1940 Ford in 1952.

entered every Grand American race (35 of them), won two of them, placed in the top five 15 times and in the top ten 23 times, and took home $18,741.00 for his trouble. In 54 other Grand American races in 1968-69, Buck won four, placed in the top five 22 times, the top ten 34 times, and has total Grand American winnings of $42,548.50.

In a Grand National career going back to 1955 (he was Grand National Champion in 1955 and 1956) Buck Baker has driven 65,454 miles in 512 races and taken home $267,477.00 in Grand National purse money.

81

Buck poses with his 1971 Pontiac Firebird.

The same car, slightly bent. Baker was unhurt.

Soapy Castles.
NASCAR

Neil "Soapy" Castles, who also makes his home in Charlotte, N.C., has won a total of $166,955.00 in Grand National racing. Soapy's in great demand as a stand-in stunt driver in Hollywood. Those who have thrilled to Elvis Presley or Rory Calhoun behind the wheel of a fast car have really been watching Soapy. In a 408-race, 53,705-mile Grand National career going back to 1957, the 37-year-old, 6-1, 180-lb. Castles has never taken a first place. But he's been in the top five 50 times, and in the top ten 168 times. Soapy has a wife and two children.

Charles L. "Chargin' Charlie" Glotzbach, of Edwardsville, Indiana, is thirty-three. The father of four entered his first Grand National race in 1960, and has since run in 68 races. He's won three, placed in the top five 25 times, the top ten 31, and driven 17,524 miles to take home $144,699. In 1968, he ran in two Grand American races, and, never closer than third place, won $1,250.00.

Charlie Glotzbach.

Goodyear

When I grow up! Chargin'
Charlie Glotzbach as a Soap Box
Racer.

Courtesy C. L. Glotzbach

Twenty-nine-year-old Peter Goodwill "Pete" Hamilton, of Dedham, Massachusetts, was 1967 Late Model Sportsman Champion. Then he moved to Grand National for the 1968 season. In 16 races, he won only $8,239.00, and in 1969, did even worse: $5,110. But 1970 was his year. He started in 16 Grand National races, and won three of them. He was in the top five 10 times, the top ten 12 times, and brought home $131,406 for the

Pete Hamilton.

NASCAR

Pete Hamilton cheerfully takes the keys to the new car he won as Rookie of the Year from Bob Pemberton, President of Air-Lift, Inc., who makes the award.

NASCAR

year. His Grand National total purse is $144,755.00. In 1969, Hamilton, six-feet-two, 175 lbs, blonde, and NAS-CAR's then most eligible bachelor (he married in 1970), entered 26 Grand American races, won twelve of them, placed in the top five 14 times, and took home Grand American purses totaling $21,743.00. He was 1968 Grand National Rookie of the Year.

James Harvey Hylton, Sr., of Inman, S.C., ran in 185

Jim Hylton.
Chrysler Corp.

Grand National races between 1964 and 1970 before
he reached the winner's circle by taking the Richmond
500 in 1969. The 36-year-old, 160-lb., 5-feet-nine-inch
driver was named Rookie of the Year in 1966. In a total of
230 races, there has been only that one first place. But
110 times, Hylton has been in the top five, and 177
times, he's been in the top ten. Over 46,382 miles, that's
been good enough to bring him $212,492.00 in Grand
National prize money. He's also run in two Grand
American races, in 1968 and 1970. He placed fifth in the
1968 race, and won $425.00. In his one 1970 race, he took
the Daytona 250 and the prize check of $5,850.00.

Bobby Isaac, the 1970 Grand National Champion, is
thirty-seven years old. He lives in Catawba, N.C., with
his wife and three children. He began racing, as a
Sportsman, in 1955. By 1961, he thought he was good
enough to try Grand National. He ran in one race, lasted
three miles, and won a total of $50.00. In the 217 other
races, he has since run, he has driven 43,086 miles. He's
won 32 Grand National races, placed in the top five 107
times, the top ten 128 times, and won a total of
$310,520.00.

Bobby Isaac (right) with
his mechanic Harry Hyde.
NASCAR

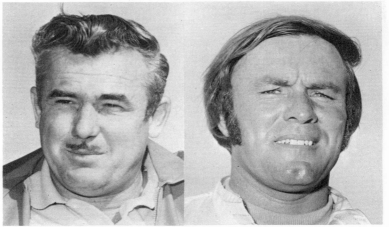

Elmo Langley.   *NASCAR* Fred Lorenzen.   *NASCAR*

Elmo Harrell Langley, 42 years old, of Landover, Maryland, has started in 358 Grand National races going back to 1955 and won only two of them. In 55,476 miles of Grand National racing, however, the father of four has won $154,347.00.

Fred Lorenzen, 37-year-old bachelor driver from Elmhurst, Illinois, was the first NASCAR driver (1963) to have won more than $100,000 in a single season. That

David Pearson.

Lorenzen looks over the engine
with master mechanic Cotton
Owens.

year, he won six of the 21 races he entered, and took
home $113,570.00. He retired from racing in 1967, but
came back in 1970. In 136 races, for a total of 31,079
miles of Grand National speeding, he's won 26 times,
placed in the top five 65 times, and in the top ten 71
times. His purses have totaled $411,558.00.

David Pearson, 37, was NASCAR Grand National
Champion in 1966, 1968 and 1969. He makes his home in
Spartanburg, S.C., with his wife and three children. Five

Pearson (left) and Petty.

Martinsville Speedway

feet eleven inches tall, weighing 185 lbs, Pearson has won 58 of the 351 Grand National races he's entered since 1960. He placed in the top five 185 times, and in the top ten 233 times. In 68,901 miles of Grand National racing, he's won $656,895.00. In addition, in one 1968 Grand American race, and four 1970 Grand American races, he earned another $3,375.00.

Richard Lee Petty, a thirty-four-year-old from Randleman, N.C., is the son of a NASCAR Hall of Fame member, Lee Petty. Six-feet-two and 195 pounds, Richard Petty is very much at home in the winner's circle. He's won 119 of the 519 Grand National races he's entered. NASCAR Grand National Driver of the Year in 1964 and 1968, Petty placed in the top five 297 times, and in the top ten 361 times, since he first began to race in the Grand Nationals in 1958 at the age of twenty-one. With total winnings of $828,908.00, Petty can well afford

Richard Petty's 1971 Plymouth Road Runner. Note mesh over side window opening.

Chrysler Corp.

Courtesy Lee Petty

When his father, Lee, was driving, 16-year-old Richard was privileged to drive the car away after the race. (April 1953.)

Dale Inman — Petty mechanic.

Mrs. Lynda Petty (left) and the kids (foreground) generally surround Richard in the Winner's Circle. This is the 1971 Daytona 500.

NASCAR

Wendell Scott (left) with George Wiltshire of Western Grand National. *NASCAR*
The only Negroes in big time NASCAR racing.

to have his wife and three children travel with him. His
brother Maurice serves as his chief mechanic, and if the
brothers have a problem, they can always seek advice
from Dad, who was Grand National Driver of the Year
himself in 1954, 1958 and 1959.

Fifty-year-old Wendell Oliver Scott, of Danville, Virginia, is the father of six. Grand National's only Negro
driver, Scott is another of those who very rarely get to the
winner's circle, even if they do make frequent trips to the
bank. In 449 races, Scott has only won one, at Jacksonville, Florida, in 1964. But in 62,490 miles of Grand
National racing, he's been close enough to the winners to
take home $151,845.00 in prize money.

John Hamilton Sears, of Ellerbe, N.C., has never made
it to the winner's circle, despite $126,278.00 in Grand
National prize money. Another father of four, 35-year-
old Sears has driven 39,482 miles in 236 races. He placed
in the top five 46 times, and in the top ten 118 times.

Grover Clifton "G.C." Spencer, of Jonesboro, Tennessee, is still another Grand National driver who hasn't
quite made it to the checkered flag and the winner's

Scott lost control at Trenton, N.J. July 11, 1970.

Scott was unhurt.

Photos:
Walter Chernokal
from NASCAR Public Relations

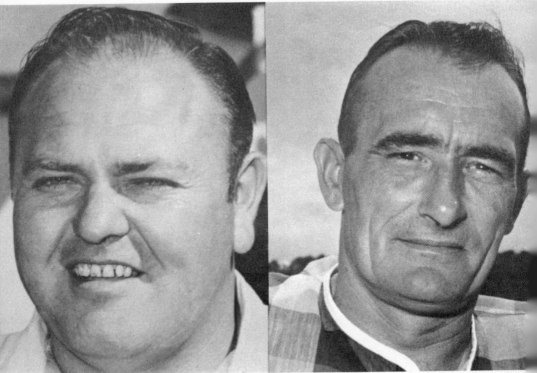

John H. Sears.   G.G. Spencer.

circle, despite 348 races and a total purse of $162,490. A
bachelor, 46 years old, Spencer has placed in the top five
53 times, and in the top ten 127 times in 48,589 miles of
racing.

William Caleb "Cale" Yarborough, thirty-two, of
Timmonsville, S.C., has won 14 of the 189 Grand
National races he's entered. This has brought him a total
of $449,961.00 in prize money, $47,250 of it from one
race, the 1968 Daytona 500.

Yarborough has placed in the top five 58 times, and in
the top ten 86 times in 39,513 miles of Grand National
racing. He's married and has one child.

94

Cale Yarborough in the Winner's Circle with his own Beauty Queen —
his wife Betty Jo. The 1968 Daytona 500.

Right on his heels is another, unrelated Yarbrough:
Thirty-three-year-old LeeRoy Yarbrough, Sr., of Colum-
bia, S.C., also has 14 Grand National wins to his credit, in
the 174 races he's entered. Coincidentally, he's also
placed in the top five 58 times. He's been in the top ten
80 times, in 36,002 miles of Grand National racing. His
purses total $407,689.00.

De Wayne "Tiny" Lund is the money king of Grand
American racing, and one of the better Grand National
racers. Forty-two years old, Lund stands six feet four and

Mrs. LeeRoy Yarbrough, LeeRoy, and Miss Union 76 in the Winner's Circle. 1969 Daytona 500.

NASCAR

NASCAR

The pit crew (including Junior Johnson, right) servicing LeeRoy's car at Daytona.

Tiny Lund and friends.

Al Cothran
from NASCAR

Frantic work by Lund's pit crew.

weighs 250 pounds. He was Grand American Champion in 1968 and 1970.

In 88 Grand American races, for 9,034 miles, Lund has taken home $79,599.50 in prize money. He's won 34 of the 88 races (in 1970 he won 19 of 35 — more than half) he entered, placed in the top five 48 times, and in the top ten 59 times.

Since 1955, Lund has run in 279 Grand National races, and won three of them. In 42,780 miles of Grand National racing, he's been in the top five 48 times, the top ten 110 times, and taken home $147,729.00 in Grand National prize money. Lund and his wife live in Cross, S.C.

There's another story about Tiny Lund, too — one

that he doesn't like to talk about. On November 11, 1963, there was a letter to Lund from a man named David B. Oliver, in Pittsburgh, Penna. It read in part, "After thorough investigation of the case, we take great pleasure in advising you that *The Carnegie Hero Fund Commission* has awarded you its Bronze Medal and the sum of $500.00 for your heroism in rescuing Mr. Marvin E. Panch from his burning race car."

Lund's response to this was that he hadn't done anything "Pancho wouldn't have done for me."

James "Jim" Paschal, 45, of High Point, N.C., another of the rare bachelors, has also turned from a fine career in Grand National racing to Grand American. He won 23 of the 325 Grand National races he entered between 1957 and 1970. He placed in the top five 130 times, and in the top ten 191 times. In 50,485 miles of Grand National racing he won $259,193.00 in prize money. In Grand American racing, he has won 15 of the 61 races he entered, placed in the top five 33 times, and in the top ten 35 times. His Grand American prize money total is $48,787.00.

Jim Paschal.

NASCAR

LeeRoy Yarbrough at Talladega.

CHAPTER SIX
The Tracks

In a book of this size, it would be impossible to list all the details of all the tracks on which NASCAR races are held. What follows is an arbitrary selection of the "Superspeedways" and some other tracks, with representative statistics.

Alabama International Motor Speedway (2.66 miles) Talladega, Alabama.
Grand National
Qualifying Record: Bobby Isaac, April 12, 1970. 1969 Dodge. 47.962 seconds. 199.658 mph.
Race Record: Pete Hamilton, August 23, 1970. 1970 Plymouth. 500 miles. 158.517 mph.

Grand American
Qualifying Record: Bunkie Blackburn, September 23, 1969. 1969 Mustang. 54.250 seconds. 176.477 mph.

99

Race Record: Ken Rush, September 13, 1969. 1968
Camaro. 400 miles. 156.271 mph.

Past Winners

Talladega 500

(1969) Richard Brickhouse	69 Dodge	153.778 mph.
(1970) Pete Hamilton	70 Plymouth	158.517 mph.

Alabama 500

(1970) Pete Hamilton	70 Plymouth	152.321 mph.

Cale Yarborough in the lead coming out of the third turn at Atlanta.   NASCAR

Atlanta International Raceway, Atlanta, Georgia.
1.552-mile.

Grand National
Qualifying Record: Buddy Baker. March 30, 1969. 1969
Dodge. 34.020 seconds. 164.226 mph.

Race Record: Richard Petty. August 2, 1970. 1970 Plymouth. 500 miles. 142.712 mph.

Grand American
Qualifying Record: Paul Goldsmith. August 3, 1968. 1968 Camaro. 36.267 seconds. 148.896 mph.

Race Record: Donnie Allison. August 3, 1968. 1968 Mustang. 250 miles. 125.302 mph.

Past Winners
Atlanta (500 miles)

(1960) Bobby Johns	60 Pontiac	108.624 mph.
(1961) Bob Burdick	61 Pontiac	124.172 mph.
* (1962) Fred Lorenzen	62 Ford	101.983 mph.
(1963) Fred Lorenzen	63 Ford	130.582 mph.
(1964) Fred Lorenzen	64 Ford	132.959 mph.
(1965) Marvin Panch	65 Ford	129.410 mph.
(1966) Jim Hurtubise	66 Plymouth	131.266 mph.
(1967) Cale Yarborough	67 Ford	131.238 mph.
(1968) Cale Yarborough	68 Mercedes	125.564 mph.
(1969) Cale Yarborough	69 Mercedes	132.191 mph.
(1970) Bobby Allison	69 Dodge	139.554 mph.

* 328 1/2 miles because of rain

Dixie 500 (500 miles)

* (1960) Fireball Roberts	60 Pontiac	112.653 mph.
(1961) David Pearson	61 Pontiac	125.384 mph.
(1962) Rex White	62 Chevrolet	124.896 mph.
(1963) Junior Johnson	63 Chevrolet	121.139 mph.
(1964) Ned Jarrett	64 Ford	112.535 mph.
(1965) Marvin Panch	65 Ford	110.120 mph.
(1966) Richard Petty	66 Plymouth	130.244 mph.
† (1967) Dick Hutcherson	67 Ford	132.286 mph.
(1968) LeeRoy Yarbrough	68 Mercedes	127.068 mph.
(1969) LeeRoy Yarbrough	69 Ford	133.001 mph.
(1970) Richard Petty	70 Plymouth	142.712 mph.

* Dixie 300

(1961 Special 250-mile race, Fred Lorenzen, 61 Ford, 118.007 mph.)
† Race changed from 400 miles to 500 miles.

Donnie Allison, shown here spinning out and moving backwards, eventually won the race — the 1970 Southern 500 at Bristol.

Bristol International Speedway

Bristol International Speedway. Bristol, Tennessee. .533-mile.

Grand National
Qualifying Record: Cale Yarborough. July 19, 1970. 1970 Mercury. 17.870 seconds. 107.375 mph.
Race Record: David Pearson. July 20, 1969. 1969 Ford. 266.5 miles. 84.043 mph.

Grand American
Qualifying Record: Bunkie Blackburn. July 20, 1968. 1968 Camaro. 21.00 seconds. 85.714 mph.
Race Record: Donnie Allison. July 20, 1968. 1968 Mustang. 150 miles. 73.210 mph.

Spare tires in the pits at Bristol.

NASCAR

Past Winners

Southeastern 500 (500 laps)

(1961) Joe Weatherly	61 Pontiac	72.45 mph.
(1962) Jim Paschal	62 Plymouth	75.28 mph.
(1963) Fireball Roberts	63 Ford	76.91 mph.
(1964) Fred Lorenzen	64 Ford	72.19 mph.
(1965) Junior Johnson	65 Ford	74.94 mph.
(1966) Dick Hutcherson	66 Ford	69.052 mph.
(1967) David Pearson	67 Dodge	75.93 mph.
(1968) David Pearson	68 Ford	77.247 mph.
(1969) Bobby Allison	69 Dodge	81.455 mph.

Volunteer 500 (500 laps)

(1961) J. Smith	61 Pontiac	68.37 mph.
(1962) B. Johns	62 Pontiac	73.32 mph.
(1963) Fred Lorenzen	63 Ford	74.84 mph.
(1964) Fred Lorenzen	64 Ford	78.04 mph.
(1965) Ned Jarrett	65 Ford	61.826 mph.
(1966) Paul Goldsmith	66 Plymouth	77.963 mph.
(1967) Richard Petty	67 Plymouth	78.705 mph.
(1968) David Pearson	68 Ford	76.310 mph.
(1969) David Pearson	69 Ford	84.043 mph.

Charlotte Motor Speedway. Charlotte, North Carolina. 1.5 mile.

Grand National
Qualifying Record: Cale Yarborough. October 12, 1969. 1969 Ford. 33.300 seconds. 162.162 mph.

Taking the checkered flag at Charlotte.

NASCAR

Race Record: Jim Paschal. May 28, 1967. 1967 Plymouth. 600 miles. 135.832 mph.

Grand American

Qualifying Record: Tiny Lund. April 12, 1970. 1969 Camaro. 35.39 seconds. 152.585 mph.

Race Record: Tiny Lund. April 12, 1970. 1969 Camaro. 250 miles. 130.488 mph.

Past Winners

World 600 (600 miles)

(1960)	Joe Lee Johnson	60 Chevrolet	107.752 mph.
(1961)	David Pearson	61 Pontiac	111.634 mph.
(1962)	Nelson Stacy	62 Ford	125.552 mph.
(1963)	Fred Lorenzen	63 Ford	132.418 mph.
(1964)	Jim Paschal	64 Plymouth	125.772 mph.
(1965)	Fred Lorenzen	65 Ford	121.772 mph.
(1966)	Marvin Panch	65 Plymouth	135.042 mph.
(1967)	Jim Paschal	67 Plymouth	135.832 mph.
*(1968)	Buddy Baker	68 Dodge	104.207 mph.
(1969)	LeeRoy Yarbrough	69 Mercedes	134.361 mph.
(1970)	Donnie Allison	69 Ford	129.680 mph.

* 382 1/2 miles because of rain

National 500 (500 miles)

(1960)	Speedy Thompson	60 Ford	112.760 mph.
(1961)	Joe Weatherly	61 Pontiac	119.800 mph.
(1962)	Junior Johnson	62 Pontiac	132.085 mph.
(1963)	Junior Johnson	63 Chevrolet	132.105 mph.
(1964)	Fred Lorenzen	64 Ford	134.559 mph.
(1965)	Fred Lorenzen	65 Plymouth	119.118 mph.
†(1966)	LeeRoy Yarbrough	66 Dodge	130.743 mph.
(1967)	Buddy Baker	67 Dodge	130.317 mph.
(1968)	Charlie Glotzbach	68 Dodge	135.324 mph.
(1969)	Donnie Allison	69 Ford	ʽ131.271 mph.
(1970)	LeeRoy Yarbrough	69 Mercedes	123.246 mph.

† Race changed from 400 miles to 500 miles

The infields and pits at Darlington.

Darlington International Speedway. Darlington, North Carolina. 1.375-mile.

(Darlington, which opened in 1949, is the first of the Superspeedways).

Grand National

Qualifying Record: Charlie Glotzbach. May 9, 1970. 1969 Dodge. 32.180 seconds. 152.814 mph.

Race Record: Richard Petty. September 4, 1967. 1967 Plymouth. 500 miles. 130.423 mph.

Grand American

Qualifying Record: Paul Goldsmith. August 31, 1968. 1968 Camaro. 34.611 seconds. 143.018 mph.

Race Record: Tiny Lund. August 31, 1968. 1968 Cougar. 250 miles. 124.296 mph.

Past Winners

Southern 500 (500 miles)

(1950)	Johnny Mantz	50 Plymouth	76.26 mph.
(1951)	Herb Thomas	51 Hudson	76.90 mph.
(1952)	Fonty Flock	52 Oldsmobile	74.51 mph.
* (1953)	Buck Baker	53 Oldsmobile	92.78 mph.
(1954)	Herb Thomas	54 Hudson	94.93 mph.
(1955)	Herb Thomas	55 Chevrolet	92.281 mph.
(1956)	Curtis Turner	56 Ford	95.067 mph.
(1957)	Speedy Thompson	57 Chevrolet	100.100 mph.
(1958)	Fireball Roberts	57 Chevrolet	102.590 mph.
(1959)	Jim Reed	59 Chevrolet	111.836 mph.
(1960)	Buck Baker	60 Pontiac	105.901 mph.
(1961)	Nelson Stacy	61 Ford	117.880 mph.
(1962)	Larry Frank	62 Ford	117.965 mph.
(1963)	Fireball Roberts	63 Ford	129.784 mph.
(1964)	Buck Baker	64 Dodge	117.757 mph.
(1965)	Ned Jarrett	65 Ford	115.924 mph.
(1966)	Darel Dieringer	66 Mercedes	114.830 mph.
(1967)	Richard Petty	67 Plymouth	130.423 mph.
(1968)	Cale Yarborough	68 Mercedes	126.132 mph.
† (1969)	LeeRoy Yarbrough	69 Ford	105.612 mph.
(1970)	Buddy Baker	69 Dodge	128.817 mph.

* Track size changed from 1 1/4 miles to 1 3/8 miles.
† 316 1/4 miles because of rain.

The fans pack in at Darlington.

NASCAR

Rebel 400 (300-400 miles)

(1957)	Fireball Roberts	57 Ford	107.940 mph.
(1958)	Curtis Turner	58 Ford	109.624 mph.
(1959)	Fireball Roberts	59 Chevrolet	115.903 mph.
(1960)	Joe Weatherly	60 Ford	102.646 mph.
(1961)	Fred Lorenzen	61 Ford	119.529 mph.
(1962)	Nelson Stacy	62 Ford	117.864 mph.
(1963)	Joe Weatherly	63 Pontiac	122.745 mph.
(1964)	Fred Lorenzen	64 Ford	130.013 mph.
(1965)	Junior Johnson	65 Ford	111.849 mph.
*(1966)	Richard Petty	66 Plymouth	131.993 mph.
(1967)	Richard Petty	67 Plymouth	125.738 mph.
(1968)	David Pearson	68 Ford	132.699 mph.
(1969)	LeeRoy Yarbrough	69 Mercedes	131.572 mph.
(1970)	David Pearson	69 Ford	129.668 mph.

* Race changed from 300 miles to 400 miles

Buddy Baker in the Winner's Circle for the 1970 Southern 500 at Darlington.

First Daytona 500 — 1959 — dead heat between Lee Petty (42) and Johnny Beauchamp (73). Top side is No. 48 Joe Weatherly, one lap behind. Probably the most thrilling race at Daytona. Petty was declared winner after many stills and movies were reviewed for several days. It appears Petty has slight edge in picture . . . but consider the angle of the finish line in the photo.

Daytona International Speedway. Daytona Beach, Florida. 2.5 miles.

Grand National

Qualifying Record: Cale Yarborough. February 22, 1970. 1969 Mercury. 46.388 seconds. 194.015 mph.

Race Record: Richard Petty. February 27, 1966. 1966 Plymouth. 500 miles (called at 495 miles because of rain). 160.627 mph.

Grand American

Qualifying Record: Tiny Lund. February 20, 1970. 1969 Camaro. (3.81-mile road course). 2 minutes 13.0 seconds. 105.821 mph.

The grandstands and infield at Daytona.

Race Record: Lloyd Ruby. July 4, 1968. 1968 Cougar. 103.152 mph.

Past Winners

Daytona 500

(1959) Lee Petty	59 Oldsmobile	135.521 mph.
(1960) Junior Johnson	59 Chevrolet	124.740 mph.
(1961) Marvin Panch	60 Pontiac	149.601 mph.
(1962) Fireball Roberts	62 Pontiac	152.529 mph.
(1963) Tiny Lund	63 Ford	151.566 mph.
(1964) Richard Petty	64 Plymouth	154.334 mph.
*(1965) Fred Lorenzen	65 Ford	141.539 mph.
†(1966) Richard Petty	66 Plymouth	160.627 mph.
(1967) Mario Andretti	67 Ford	146.926 mph.
(1968) Cale Yarborough	68 Mercedes	143.251 mph.
(1969) LeeRoy Yarbrough	69 Ford	157.950 mph.
(1970) Pete Hamilton	70 Plymouth	149.601 mph.

* 332 1/2 miles because of rain
† 495 miles because of rain

110

Firecracker 400

(1959)	Fireball Roberts	59 Pontiac	140.581 mph.
(1960)	Jack Smith	60 Pontiac	146.842 mph.
(1961)	David Pearson	61 Pontiac	154.294 mph.
(1962)	Fireball Roberts	62 Pontiac	153.688 mph.
*(1963)	Fireball Roberts	63 Ford	150.927 mph.
(1964)	A.J. Foyt	64 Dodge	151.451 mph.
(1965)	A.J. Foyt	65 Ford	150.046 mph.
(1966)	Sam McQuagg	66 Dodge	153.813 mph.
(1967)	Cale Yarborough	67 Ford	143.583 mph.
(1968)	Cale Yarborough	68 Mercedes	167.247 mph.
(1969)	LeeRoy Yarbrough	69 Ford	160.875 mph.
(1970)	Donnie Allison	69 Ford	162.235 mph.

* Race changed from 250 miles to 400 miles

chematic drawing of Daytona.

Daytona Speedway Corp.

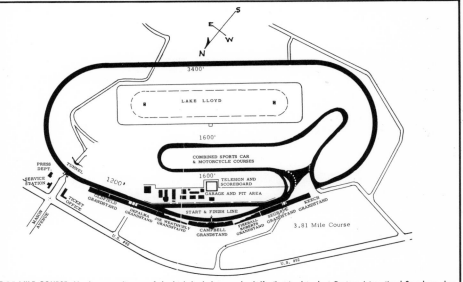

THE 2.5 MILE COURSE: Here's a new diagram of the high banked two and a half mile trioval track at Daytona International Speedway, show-
the "D" shape with 31 degree banks in both the east and west turns and an 18 inch bank just in front of Campbell grandstand. This shows the
dition of the new grandstands with the Fireball Roberts grandstand replacing the Segrave Annex.

Dover Downs from the air.

Dover Downs International Speedway. Dover, Delaware. 1.0 mile.

Grand National
Qualifying Record: David Pearson. July 6, 1969. 1969 Ford. 27.601 seconds. 130.430 mph.
Race Record: Richard Petty. June 26, 1969. 1969 Ford. 300 miles. 115.772 mph.

Grand American
Qualifying Record: Tiny Lund. May 31, 1970. 1969 Camaro. 27.71 seconds. 129.916 mph.
Race Record: Ken Rush. May 31, 1970. 1969 Camaro. 250 miles. 116.928 mph.

Martinsville Speedway. Martinsville, Virginia. .525-mile.

Grand National
Qualifying Record: David Pearson. September 28, 1969. 1969 Ford. 21.635 seconds. 87.358 mph.
Race Record: Richard Petty. October 18, 1970. 1970 Plymouth. 262.5 miles. 72.159 mph.

Grand American
Qualifying Record: Not available.
Race Record: Jim Paschal. October 17, 1970. 1970 Javelin. 52.5 miles (100 laps). 62.151 mph.

The first turn at Martinsville Speedway.

NASCAR

Michigan's Irish Hills from the air.

Grand American cars coming out of Irish Hills' second turn.

The grandstands at Irish Hills.

Irish Hills.

Michigan International Speedway. Irish Hills, Michigan. 2.04 miles.

Grand National

Qualifying Record: Pete Hamilton. June 7, 1970. 1970 Plymouth. 44.243 seconds. 165.992 mph.

Race Record: Charlie Glotzbach. August 16, 1970. 1969 Dodge. 400 miles. 147.571 mph.

Grand American

Qualifying Record: Pete Hamilton. August 16, 1969. 1969 Camaro. 47.385 seconds. 151.946 mph.

Race Record: Ken Rush. August 16, 1969. 1968 Camaro. 250 miles. 115.890 mph.

Past Winners

Motor State 400

(1969) Cale Yarborough	69 Mercedes	139.254 mph.
*(1970) Cale Yarborough	69 Mercedes	138.302 mph.

* Race changed from 500 to 400 miles

Yankee 400

*(1969) David Pearson	69 Ford	115.508 mph.
†(1970) Charlie Glotzbach	69 Dodge	147.571 mph.

* 330 miles because of rain.

† Race changed from 500 to 400 miles

Rockingham from the air.

North Carolina Motor Speedway. Rockingham, North Carolina. 1.017-mile.

Grand National
Qualifying Record: Bobby Allison. March 8, 1970. 1969 Dodge. 26.329 seconds. 139.048 mph.
Race Record: Cale Yarborough. November 15, 1970. 1969 Mercury. 500 miles. 119.811 mph.

Grand American
Qualifying Record: Tiny Lund. March 9, 1968. 1968 Cougar. 113.996 mph.
Race Record: Tiny Lund. March 9, 1968. 1968 Cougar. 250 miles. 95.857 mph.

Past Winners

American 500 (500 miles)

(1965) Curtis Turner	65 Ford	101.943 mph.
(1966) Fred Lorenzen	66 Ford	104.348 mph.
(1967) Bobby Allison	67 Ford	99.420 mph.
(1968) Richard Petty	68 Plymouth	105.060 mph.
(1969) LeeRoy Yarbrough	69 Ford	111.938 mph.
(1970) Cale Yarborough	69 Mercedes	119.811 mph.

Carolina 500 (500 miles)

(1966) Paul Goldsmith	66 Plymouth	100.072 mph.
(1967) Richard Petty	67 Plymouth	104.682 mph.
(1968) Donnie Allison	68 Ford	99.338 mph.
(1969) David Pearson	69 Ford	102.569 mph.
(1970) Richard Petty	70 Plymouth	116.117 mph.

James Hylton hit wall and was hit by several cars in pileup in American 500 at N.C. Motor Speedway in Rockingham, N.C., in October, 1967. His shoulder harness, which had been used all year, separated at seam. He suffered concussion and was in hospital 6 days.

NASCAR

Hylton's car after the wreck.

NASCAR

North Wilkesboro Speedway.

North Wilkesboro Speedway. North Wilkesboro, North Carolina. .625 mile.

Grand National
Qualifying Record: Bobby Isaac. April 18, 1970. 1969 Dodge. 21.020 seconds. 107.040 mph.
Race Record: Bobby Allison. April 20, 1969. 1969 Dodge. 250 miles. 95.268 mph.

Grand American
Qualifying Record: Tiny Lund. September 28, 1968. 1968 Cougar. 21.793 seconds. 92.958 mph.
Race Record: Tiny Lund. September 28, 1968. 1968 Cougar. 150 miles. 92.958 mph.

Two ways to go — Cal Yarborough (21) leads the field of stock cars up through the Riverside Esses, while A.J. Foyt (27) (upper right) explores some of the terrain outside the turn during the 1970 Motor Trend-Riverside 500 action.

Riverside International Raceway

Riverside International Speedway. Riverside, California. 2.62 miles.

Grand National
Qualifying Record: Parnelli Jones. January 18, 1970. 1970 Ford. 1 minute 23.211 seconds. 113.310 mph.

Race Record: Richard Petty. February 1, 1969. 1969 Ford. 500 miles. 105.498 mph.

Does not run *Grand American*

119

Past Winners

Riverside 500

(1963) Dan Gurney	63 Ford	84.965 mph.
(1964) Dan Gurney	64 Ford	91.154 mph.
(1965) Dan Gurney	65 Ford	87.708 mph.
(1966) Dan Gurney	66 Ford	97.946 mph.
(1967) Parnelli Jones	67 Ford	91.080 mph.
(1968) Dan Gurney	68 Ford	100.598 mph.
(1969) Richard Petty	69 Ford	105.516 mph.
(1970) A.J. Foyt	70 Ford	97.450 mph.

Falstaff 400

(1970) Richard Petty	70 Plymouth	101.120 mph.

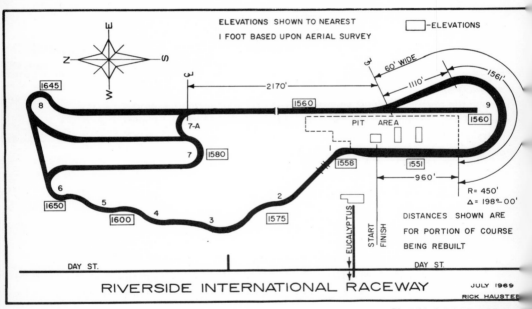

RIVERSIDE INTERNATIONAL RACEWAY

CHAPTER SEVEN
The Hall of Fame

The National Motorsports Press Association, a professional organization whose members report NASCAR racing wherever it is held, are probably in the best position to judge those involved in the sport.

The NMPA's main project is the selection of drivers, owners, and others who have made major contributions to NASCAR racing for the Stock Car Racing Hall of Fame. This book would be incomplete if it did not include the Hall of Fame.

GLENN "FIREBALL" ROBERTS
1928-1964

The greatest stock car racer of all time, Roberts, who died of burns suffered in the World 600 at Charlotte, N.C., in 1964, is buried within sound of the cars at Daytona.

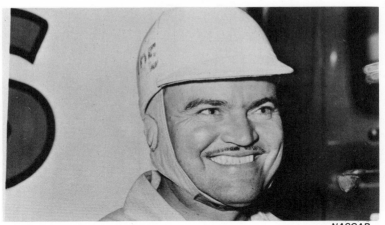

NASCAR

TRUMAN FONTELLO "FONTY" FLOCK
Driver

NASCAR

JOE HERBERT "LITTLE JOE" WEATHERLY
Driver
"THE CLOWN PRINCE OF RACING"

MARSHALL TEAGUE
Driver

NASCAR

ROBERT "RED" BYRON
Driver

NASCAR

LEE ARNOLD PETTY
Driver, Mechanic, Owner

NASCAR

PAUL McDUFFIE
Mechanic

NASCAR

ROBERT E. "BOB" COLVIN
Promoter
1907-1967

HERB THOMAS
Driver

JAMES A. "PAT" PURCELL
Official
1906-1966

BILLY MEYERS
Driver
1924-1958

E.G. "CANNONBALL" BAKER
Driver
First NASCAR Commissioner
1891-1960

EVERETT "COTTON" OWENS
Driver-Mechanic-Owner

National Association
for
Stock Car Auto Racing
Inc.

BILL FRANCE
President

WILLIAM C. FRANCE
Vice President

LIN KUCHLER
Vice President
Competition Director

RUSS MOYER
Executive Manager

PHIL HOLMER
Public Relations Director

Copyright 1971 by
National Association for
Stock Car Auto Racing, Inc.

P. O. BOX K
DAYTONA BEACH, FLA. 32015

RB 1/1/71

127

INDEX

	Section	Page
Adjudication	15	24
Appeals	16	25
Benefit Plan	3	8
Cadet Class Specifications	20E	88
Entry Regulations	5	10
Federation de l'Automobile	19	34
Flag Rules	13	19
Fuel Cell	Rear Pages	
Grand American Specifications	20A	51
Grand National Specifications	20	35
Hobby Specifications	20E	82
Inspections	6	11
Late Model Hobby Specifications	20E	86
Late Model Sportsman Specifications	20B	63
Late Model Sportsman Regulations (Superspeedways)	20C	72
Licenses	2	5
Limited Sportsman Class	20F	92
Membership	1	4
Modified Specifications	20D	75
National Commissioner	16A	26
National Stock Car Racing Commission	16	25
Other Divisions	20G	92
Performance Trials	11	19
Point Funds	18	28
Prize Money	17	27
Protests	15	24
Race Procedure	9	16
Race Regulations	7	11
Refueling Can	Rear Pages	
Roll Bar Diagrams	Rear Pages	
Safety Regulations	8	14
Sanctioned Events	4	9
Seat Diagrams	Rear Pages	
Special Rules	10	18
Special Tests	12	19
Violations	14	21

FOREWORD

This 1971 edition of the NASCAR rules and regulations has been compiled and published after careful study by your NASCAR officials and consultation with competitors in all divisions. We feel it is the best set of rules possible for our sport.

Beginning with 1971, NASCAR is encouraging a move to reduce the cost of competition through the utilization of more easily accessible parts and equipment. By bringing down the costs, we also plan to have more competitive cars in an event than ever before.

For the new season there is one formal name change. The Pacific Coast Late Model division has been changed to the Western Grand National division.

There are some minor changes made in the 1971 rules and we suggest you study the entire book in order to become more attuned to all aspects of NASCAR racing.

Another change involves 1971 ACCUS-FIA car classification The ACCUS-FIA Car Classification committee has developed a formula which gives manufacturers an incentive to better streamline the lower priced Intermediate size cars.

Every organization, to be successful, must have good rules and must enforce them fairly. We think your 1971 rules are fair for all competitors. We have, as usual, concentrated on safety.

It is up to you, the competitors who use this book, to see that these rules benefit everyone in the sport.

We at NASCAR wish all of you a successful year.

BILL FRANCE,
President

To insure the safety of participants in automobile stock car racing, as well as that of the spectators, and to provide for the orderly conduct of stock car racing events, requires close adherence to the rules and regulations hereinafter set forth. All members of NASCAR agree to comply with these rules.

SECTION 1 — MEMBERSHIP

1. Any individual interested in automobile stock car racing may become a member of NASCAR by filing an application, agreeing to abide by these rules and paying the fee prescribed for membership, provided he meets the required qualifications.

2. NASCAR MEMBERSHIP IS DIVIDED INTO THE FOLLOWING CLASSES:

a. Grand National Championship division. (Includes Western Grand National).
b. Grand American division.
c. Late Model Sportsman division.
d. Modified division.
e. Hobby division, including Late Model Hobby, Cadet class and Limited Sportsman.
f. Industrial.
g. Race Official.
h. Non-competitive (Fan).

3. ANNUAL MEMBERSHIP DUES IN NASCAR SHALL BE AS FOLLOWS:

a. Grand National (Includes Western Grand National) (driver, car owner or mechanic) $35
b. Grand American (driver, car owner or mechanic) 35
c. Late Model Sportsman (driver, car owner or mechanic) 30
d. Modified (driver, car owner or mechanic) 30
e. Stock Car (Northern California) (driver, car owner or mechanic) 30
f. Hobby (driver, car owner or mechanic) 25

(1) In each of the foregoing divisions, full fee is required for each additional membership in same name.
(2) Car owners are required to have separate membership for each division in which they compete.
(3) Driver memberships in Grand National and Western Grand National divisions also valid for Late Model Sportsman and Modified divisions except as provided by Section 2 paragraph 3, of these rules with respect to drivers.
(4) Driver memberships in Grand American division also valid for Late Model Sportsman and Modified divisions except as provided by Section 2, Paragraph 3, of these rules with respect to drivers.
(5) Mechanic memberships in Grand National, Western Grand

National and Grand American divisions valid for all divisions except Hobby.
(6) Driver and mechanic memberships in Late Model Sportsman and Modified divisions are valid for those divisions only.
(7) Driver and mechanic memberships in the Hobby Division are valid for that division only.
g. Industrial $35
h. Race Official 30
i. Non-competitive (Fan) 15

4. NASCAR members are not employees of NASCAR and are independent contractors, and assume and take all responsibility for all charges, premiums, and taxes, if any, payable on any funds they may receive as a result of their participation in any events as members of NASCAR.

5. NASCAR memberships are issued only by NASCAR Headquarters after receipt of a proper application and payment of the requisite dues. Acceptance of a membership application and fee by any NASCAR Official does not constitute approval of a NASCAR license application. All license applications must be approved by NASCAR Headquarters in Daytona Beach, Fla.

6. NASCAR is dedicated to the highest degree of safety and sportsmanlike conduct in stock car automobile racing and all members are required to conduct themselves in such a manner as to promote this end.

7. Only those individuals approved by NASCAR (including but not necessarily limited to necessary fire, wrecker, ambulance and security crews) shall have access to or be allowed in the pit or garage areas during an event, and the Promoter and Operating Corporation shall provide sufficient security personnel in the pit and garage areas to enforce this provision at all times during the event.

SECTION 2 — LICENSES

1. Any member of NASCAR who participates in any NASCAR sanctioned event as a driver, car owner, mechanic, or official, or industrial representative, must possess a valid NASCAR license authorizing participation as such.

2. All licenses will be issued without charge by NASCAR Headquarters on receipt of a completed, authentic NASCAR membership application form, required membership dues, signed Benefit Plan Registration and Indemnity Agreement and properly executed Minor's Release if applicant is under 21 years of age.

3. NASCAR reserves the right to approve or reject any and all license applications. Only holders of Grand American licenses may drive and compete in NASCAR sanctioned Grand American

events, provided, however, that in the event the holder of a Grand National license desires to compete in a particular NASCAR sanctioned Grand American event, he shall make application therefor to the Competition Director of NASCAR well in advance of the event and the Director of Competition, if he determines that the participation of the Grand National licensee will not unduly affect the competitive balance of the entrants in the particular event, may waive this provision of these rules and permit the Grand National licensee to participate in the event. NASCAR licenses are reviewed from month to month, and automatically renewed if approved by NASCAR. NASCAR reserves the right to terminate any license at the end of any month by written notice to the member. Members may discontinue their NASCAR membership at any time by surrendering their competition licenses, accompanied by their letter of resignation, to NASCAR Headquarters in Daytona Beach, Fla.

4. No license will be issued until a fully completed and signed Benefit Plan Registration Release and indemnity Agreement has been received at NASCAR Headquarters. Any applicant for a license who is under 21 years of age must have the Minor's Release on the membership and license application signed by both living parents and both signatures must be witnessed. If only one parent is living, the Minor's Release must carry that parent's signature which must be witnessed. If both parents are not living, the Minor's Release must be signed by a court-appointed legal guardian and must be accompanied by a certified copy of the court order which names him as the applicant's legal guardian. The signature of the legal guardian also must be witnessed.

5. A license can be used only by the member to whom it is issued and any member who allows any other person to use, or attempt to use, his license in any manner shall be subject to disciplinary action as hereinafter provided.

6. TO SECURE A NASCAR LICENSE AS A RACE DRIVER, A MEMBER MUST:

a. Hold a valid automobile driver's license in his home state, and be at least 16 years of age, or the minimum age required by the law of the state in which he competes.

b. Submit to and pass driving ability tests conducted by and at the discretion of NASCAR officials, whose decision as to driving ability is final and binding on the applicant.

c. Submit to a physical examination when this is deemed necessary by NASCAR officials and be certified by the examining physician as being physically fit for race driving.

d. The possession of an FIA license is a requisite for eligibility to participate in FIA-approved events. The FIA rule in this regard states...

FIA PROVISIONAL COMPETITION RULES FOR DRIVERS' LICENSES

V-7. Conditions of an FIA license: The possession of an FIA license is a requisite for eligibility to participate in FIA-approved events. The member Club is empowered to issue an FIA license.

ACCUS-FIA may refuse to issue a license without stating any reason for such refusal. Furthermore, it may suspend or revoke a license in accordance with the provisions of the FIA Code following a hearing of the circumstances in accordance with appeal procedures published by the ACCUS-FIA Board or a committee appointed by the Board. In addition, the member clubs — NASCAR, SCCA, USAC and NHRA — may suspend, revoke or refuse to renew an FIA license held by a person under suspension by his member club.

The four member organizations must notify ACCUS-FIA immediately when one of their drivers has his club competition license withdrawn.

V-8. Acceptance or refusal of entries: The possession of an FIA license in no way guarantees the holder a blanket acceptance to compete. A sanctioning body has every right to solicit entries by invitation to FIA licenseholders regardless of their club affiliation. Conversely, a sanctioning body may refuse or exclude any entrant or driver without stating any reason. This refusal is final and without appeal, but notification of refusal must be made by the sanctioning body within 8 days of receipt of entry and not less than 4 days before commencement of the event, unless the Supplementary Regulations state otherwise.

7. TO SECURE A NASCAR LICENSE AS A CAR OWNER, A MEMBER MUST:

a. Be at least 16 years of age, or the minimum age required by the law of the state in which he competes.

b. All cars taking part in NASCAR events must be registered and licensed at NASCAR Headquarters, regardless of whether or not a licensed driver owns a car.

c. Car numbers will be assigned by NASCAR Headquarters. Whenever possible, requested number will be assigned but NASCAR reserves the right to issue all numbers in order to prevent duplication and maintain proper records.

d. In event a car is owned by a partnership or corporation, license will be issued to one person only. But corporate name may also appear on the membership application and license, and all point fund money will be issued in the name of the corporation.

e. Owner of a registered car may transfer license to a replace-

f. No license is transferable except as in sub-paragraph "e" immediately above.

g. If a licensed car is sold, new owner shall file a car registration application and a new license and car number will be issued.

h. If a licensed car is sold, new owner may be allowed to use the old car number with written permission of original registered owner.

i. When a registered car is sold, NASCAR shall be notified immediately and to whom car has been sold. Violation of rules relative to any car sold without notice to NASCAR will subject original registrant to suspension, and/or loss of points.

i. Car owners with more than one car must register all cars and use the numbers assigned by NASCAR.

k. NASCAR assumes no responsibility in event of error in scoring or point tabulation if number other than that officially assigned is used.

l. It is not necessary for licensed car owner to secure additional mechanic's license.

m. All car owners entering NASCAR-FIA listed events must possess a current valid FIA Entrant's license.

8. TO SECURE A NASCAR LICENSE AS A MECHANIC, A MEMBER MUST:

a. Be at least 16 years of age, or the minimum age required by the law of the state in which he competes.

b. Submit to a physical examination when this is deemed necessary by NASCAR officials and be certified by the examining physician as being physically fit for race mechanic.

9. THE FOLLOWING PROCEDURES GOVERN USE OF LICENSES AT NASCAR SANCTIONED EVENTS:

a. Drivers and car owners, when signing in for any event, must turn in NASCAR license to NASCAR official in charge.

b. Licenses will be returned when drivers receive prize money or at time and place specified by NASCAR officials in charge.

c. License of competitors injured in, or suspended during running of event will be forwarded to NASCAR Headquarters and returned upon proof of ability to drive or lifting of suspension.

SECTION 3. — BENEFIT PLAN

1. Each NASCAR member with a competitor permit, and who has signed the release sheet for the meet for which the competitor permit is issued, is entitled to benefits as arranged by NASCAR if he is accidentally injured, the result of external violent and visible means, while participating in said meet. All competitors in NASCAR sanctioned events agree to abide by the decisions of the Benefit Plan officials in administering the Benefit Plan. The Benefit Plan applies only at NASCAR sanctioned events and not while en route to or from a racemeet.

2. No member will be allowed in the pit area until he or she has secured a competitor permit—and signed the release sheet for that particular meet.

3. Competitors' permits are not transferable and are not to be signed by anyone except the person to whom issued.

4. Any member returning to his usual occupation or competition after injury shall be deemed to be physically fit and further disability benefits shall cease as of that date.

5. Any member involved in an accident while on the racing premises and who does not report to the NASCAR official in charge before leaving the premises (providing such member is able to make such a report) will not be eligible for benefits prescribed under the Benefit Plan.

6. The 1971 Benefit Plan schedule is as follows:

a. Total disablement, $1,560.00 — This will be paid at the rate of $60.00 each week, starting from the eighth day, but not exceeding altogether 26 consecutive weeks for any single disablement which prevents the NASCAR member from engaging in his usual occupation or any racing events. (Disablement must begin within 30 days of accident).

b. Blanket medical, $15,000.00 — Including expense of treatment by a physician, surgeon, chiropractor, osteopath, nurses, hospital and other professional services rendered and payment may be made directly to these people for the account of the injured NASCAR member. (Treatment must commence within 26 weeks of accident).

c. Death, $15,000.00 will be paid to the named beneficiary, less reasonable funeral and burial expenses which the Benefit Plan of the Competitor Liaison Bureau of NASCAR, Inc. is authorized to pay.

d. Dismemberment or loss of both arms, legs or sight of eyes, $15,000.00. Loss of one arm, leg or sight of eye $7,500.00. (Maximum $15,000.00.)
(Loss under sub-paragraphs c or d must occur within 9 months of date of accident, and payment of benefits under either item will preclude payment under the other.)

SECTION 4 — SANCTIONED EVENTS

1. Only NASCAR members who are properly licensed by NASCAR are authorized to participate in racing events which are officially sanctioned by NASCAR.

2. Applications for official NASCAR sanctions must be directed to NASCAR Headquarters. Such application must be completed in full and filed with NASCAR Headquarters at least three weeks before a scheduled event or the first race of the season for tracks operating on a weekly or other regular schedule.

3. Sanctions will be granted and issued only by NASCAR Headquarters.

4. Grand National, Western Grand National, Grand American and Special Events require a separate sanction application and approval for each event, and must be filed at NASCAR Headquarters at least three weeks before the date of each event.

5. Special Events include (1) team events, (2) sectional, state and national championships, (3) combination programs, or (4) a feature event which is run over a greater distance and for a larger purse than is customarily presented at the track in question in its established weekly programs.

SECTION 5 — ENTRY REGULATIONS

1. Any driver or car owner who fails to file an entry before deadline listed on entry blank will receive prize money won in racemeet but will not be credited with NASCAR points or multiple for the event. Drivers and owners may file separate or combined entry blanks to be eligible for points except in Grand National, Western Grand National, Grand American or any other events governed by special entry regulations as defined in paragraph 4 of this section.

2. Entry blank must contain all requested information, including the signatures of the driver and car owner.

3. Under no circumstances will a driver or car owner who files an entry, or in any way informs a promoter, track operator or NASCAR Headquarters that he will run in a racemeet on a given day, be excused from competing in that meet without the consent of the NASCAR Competition Director, and it shall be the responsibility of the car owner to have his assigned driver ready to run. (Promoter or track operator must furnish NASCAR with official signed entry blank for the event in question). (Penalties for violation of this rule are shown in Section 14, paragraph k and sub-paragraph k(1) of these rules).

4. For Grand National, Western Grand National, Grand American or any other events governed by special entry regulations, no driver's entry will be accepted if his entry form does not include his valid signature and the car owner's entry and car owner's valid signature, or a car owner's entry, with car owner's valid signature, verifying that the driver in question has a car entered for his use. To be eligible for NASCAR championship points and race multiple, driver and/or car owner entries must be submitted before the official entry closing date as verified by the U.S. postal date stamp if mailed, or NASCAR date stamp if delivered in person to NASCAR, Daytona Beach, Fla. No telegraph or telephone entries will be accepted.

5. Any driver and/or car owner participating in any NASCAR sanctioned event without having submitted to NASCAR a signed entry blank will be governed by all special rules and/or releases appearing on said entry blank; and in the event the entry blank includes an advertising release said driver and/or car owner shall not have any claim for damages and/or special recompense for any subsequent advertising exploiting achievements or any product used by the driver and/or the car in said event.

6. For all Grand National, Western Grand National, Grand American and Special Events, promoter and/or track operator agree to abide by all entry regulations and conditions drafted and published by NASCAR as they may appear on the published entry blank for a specific racemeet. Failure of promoter and/or track operator to comply with this rule will result in cancellation of sanction.

SECTION 6 — INSPECTIONS

1. The method and type of car inspection, and number of cars to be inspected, at any NASCAR racemeet or event may be determined by NASCAR official in charge or by order of NASCAR officers.

2. NASCAR reserves the right for inspection purposes to seal or impound cars competing in a sanctioned event.

3. NASCAR assumes no responsibility for impounded cars.

4. NASCAR reserves the right to limit admittance to any area or garage in which inspections are being made; and the NASCAR Official in charge has the right to limit the attendance to only the NASCAR Inspectors and two mechanics assigned to handle the work necessary in preparing the car for the inspection.

5. NASCAR reserves the right to confiscate any part and/or equipment that does not meet NASCAR specifications.

6. NASCAR specifically reserves the right to inspect any car which has previously participated in a race not sanctioned by NASCAR to determine that it meets all safety standards required in NASCAR sanctioned events.

SECTION 7 — RACE REGULATIONS

1. Drinking of alcoholic beverages or the use of any type of stimulating or tranquilizing drug is strictly forbidden on the racing premises. Any participant in a NASCAR event who shows evidence of having partaken of any alcoholic beverage or, upon medical examination, of having used any stimulating or tranquilizing drug must leave the premises immediately and will be subject to penalty as outlined in Section 14, paragraph 3e.

2. Promoter, Race Director or NASCAR officials may refuse to accept entry of any car or driver.

3. NASCAR officials have the right to temporarily change race car numbers to avoid duplication.

4. All changes in type of race program, including time trials, must

...approved by NASCAR Headquarters, except in the case of regular weekly one day events.

5. No driver or crew member may enter racing area until he has personally signed all required releases, registrations and entry forms. No person will be permitted at any time to sign the release sheet for anyone other than himself.

6. No changes of driver at any time shall be made without proper notification to NASCAR officials. When race is in progress, changes must be made in pits only.

7. At all racemeets the driver assumes responsibility for actions of his pit crew in every respect. The driver shall be the sole spokesman for his car owner and pit crew in any and all matters pertaining to the race and must talk to the NASCAR official in charge. In national championship events, the driver must inform the NASCAR official in charge the name of his pit captain, who shall have the sole right to represent him while driver is in actual competition or should the driver be incapacitated.

8. No licensed member shall subject any official to abuse or improper language at any time.

9. Decisions of NASCAR race officials on interpretation of rules pertaining to race procedure or scoring of positions shall be considered final.

a. When score sheets are sent to NASCAR Headquarters for re-check, they must be accompanied by $100 service fee to be posted by the individual requesting the re-check.

10. No driver, car owner or mechanic shall have any claim for damages, expenses or otherwise against promoter, track operator, NASCAR's officers, directors, officials, agents or employees by reason of disqualification, or damage to, either car or driver or both; and they agree the track is in a safe and usable condition if they take part in the racing activities.

11. NASCAR officials have the right to subject any driver to a physical examination before he is allowed to compete.

12. NASCAR reserves the right to subject any car to a mechanical inspection at the discretion of the NASCAR Technical Inspector or NASCAR official in charge of the event.

a. It shall be the responsibility of the driver or car owner to tear-down a car for inspection when requested to do so by the said Technical Inspector or NASCAR official in charge of the event. Failure to comply will result in disqualification of driver and car.

13. At any event which calls for a mandatory inspection of cars after a racemeet, any car taken from the racing premises without permission from the NASCAR official in charge, or that is not taken immediately to the inspection station after receiving permission to leave the racing premises, will subject the driver and the car to dis-

qualification unless it can be proven beyond any reasonable doubt that the violation was caused by circumstances over which the car owner or driver could not have any control.

14. After a protest is made on engine specifications, an engine cooling period of 30 minutes shall be allowed. If after this time limit, the competitor has not started dismantling engine, the car will be disqualified.

15. Gambling is prohibited at any NASCAR-sanctioned event.

16. NASCAR members shall not take part or participate in any action or activity considered detrimental to NASCAR or stock car racing.

17. NASCAR members shall not participate in fights on race premises at any time.

18. NASCAR members agree to abide by official NASCAR decisions.

19. NASCAR reserves the right to have all cars use same grade and brand of gasoline at any event.

20. All drivers, car owners and/or mechanics assume full responsibility for any and all injuries sustained, including death and property damage, any time they are on racing premises, en route thereto or therefrom.

21. Safety inspectors positively forbid the use of any vehicle in the pits or racing area to be used for spectator vantage positions. No one will be allowed to sit or stand on top of any service vehicle or truck in the pits or racing area. Individual owners and/or managers of such vehicles will be held responsible by NASCAR, and any violation of this regulation may result in expulsion from the pits or racing area.

22. NASCAR official in charge of the event will be the senior NASCAR official present at the race course, or as assigned by NASCAR. All official personnel will be directly responsible to the ranking NASCAR official in charge of the event. Chief Steward at any event shall not act as the official starter at that event.

23. All disputes developing as a result of local track rules must be settled at the track; NASCAR Headquarters will not accept protests based on local track rules or regulations.

24. West Coast members and officials must refer requests for rulings on local protests to NASCAR district field managers:

Northern California —   Bob Barkhimer
14 Camp Evers Lane
Santa Cruz, California 95060

Southern California, —   Art Atkinson
Nevada and Arizona   2850 East Colorado Boulevard
Pasadena, California 91107

Washington & Oregon—Bill Amick
4412 N. E. 86th Avenue
Portland, Oregon 97220
—Pete Keller

Western   2850 East Colorado Boulevard
Grand National   Pasadena, California 91107
Division Director

SECTION 8 — SAFETY REGULATIONS

Accessories used in the interest of safety and car handling will be considered for approval and minimum and maximum tolerance will be established after any accessory has been approved.

The following shall cover all types of racing, speed trials or special tests where an element of danger is involved:

1. A quick release approved type safety belt of no less than three (3) inches width shall be compulsory. Both ends must be fastened to roll bar cage with aircraft quality bolts not less than 3/8 of an inch diameter. A steel plate may be welded to the roll bar cage on the right side of the driver so the belt can be brought down in such a manner that it will prevent the driver from sliding from side to side under the belt. The belt must come from behind the driver.

It is recommended that safety belt clasps be secured by locking with tape, twine or a heavy rubber band.

2. Helmets must be full head coverage type and must meet the American Standards Association Z90.1-1966 testing standards. To be eligible for use in NASCAR competition, the manufacturer of any model helmet must furnish NASCAR with certification that the helmet in question has been tested according to ASA requirements.

3. Shoulder harness and additional V-type seat belt mandatory. NASCAR-approved padded head rest mandatory.

4. All cars are subject to inspection at any time before taking part in a sanctioned racemeet, speed trial or special tests. It is the sole responsibility of a driver, car owner or mechanic to have his car free from mechanical defects and in safe racing condition.

a. Additions to car bodies, such as fins, wings, scoops, signs, etc., will not be permitted in regular racing; but may be approved for use in special experimental tests.

5. No driver shall compete in any event with head or arm extended outside of a closed body race car.

6. No race, time trial or warm-up, shall be started unless the following equipment is on the premises (and it is the responsibility of the promoter to see that the equipment is provided):

(a) An ambulance and attendant whose minimum requirements shall be having satisfactorily completed an accredited First Aid course such as the one given by the Red Cross.

(b) A properly manned fire truck equipped with carbon dioxide and/or dry powder type extinguishers or a fire truck with fog spray equipment.

(c) Two wreckers, one equipped with emergency equipment.

7. No race cars shall be allowed on track unless the official starter, assigned by the NASCAR official in charge, is at the starter's position.

8. All drivers, car owners or mechanics when running car around

high quality racing helmet and have a safety belt, shoulder harness and additional V-type seat belt, and must have all doors on car properly secured.

9. No car shall carry more than one person any time during a race, practice or warm-up. A driver shall not permit any person to ride on any part of his car at any time car is in racing area.

(a) Any cameras mounted in any cars, by special NASCAR permission, must be mounted in a manner approved by the Chief NASCAR Technical Inspector.

10. Race cars must have an approved-type fire extinguisher securely mounted within driver's reach, and each pit crew should have an approved-type fire extinguisher with its equipment within ready reach for any emergency.

11. Center-top of steering post must be padded with at least two inches of a resilient material.

12. Elevated gasoline drums or refueling towers will not be allowed. Only approved ventilated gasoline cans, equipped with a flexible filter nozzle and/or tube, will be permitted. All cans limited to 11-gallon maximum capacity. Only two 11-gallon capacity cans permitted in each pit. Filler can capacity must appear in 3-inch painted letters on side of all filler cans. POSITIVELY NO FUNNELS.

13. USE OF TWO (2) GASOLINE CANS AT THE SAME TIME WHILE REFUELING WILL NOT BE PERMITTED—violation will mean instant disqualification.

14. Not more than 30 gallons of gasoline per car will be allowed in any one pit at any time.

15. When tires are changed on a pit stop, all lug nuts must be replaced and tightened on that stop. Violators will be held in the pits for one lap.

16. When making a pit stop, only five (5) men will be allowed over the wall, except in the Grand American division which is restricted to two (2) men over the wall. No manufacturers personnel will be permitted over the wall at any time during the running of a race. A 15-second penalty will be imposed, at the time of the infraction of this provision, on a competing car each time more than five of the car's pit crew are over the pit wall at the same time during an event.

17. Drivers must, at all times, wear driving suits that effectively cover the body from neck to ankles and wrists. Suits must be manufactured from fire resistant material.

SECTION 9 — RACE PROCEDURE

1. No driver may qualify more than one car in time trials or qualifying races. The time accredited to each car determines its starting position.

   a. In national championship events, the fastest qualifier will be given his choice of starting on the pole or taking the outside position in the front row. The fastest qualifier will be used as the control car for the start.

   b. In postponed events where requalifying is specified, only the qualifying times established in requalifying will be certified as NASCAR records.

2. Any qualified car may be driven in any race by any eligible driver. A driver may get out of one car and drive another, but after driving the second car, he may not get back into the first car except in races 100 miles or longer.

3. Time trials or a handicap point system may be used to determine starting positions. The method used should be agreed upon by officials and promoter, and should be brought to the attention of all competitors before the race program starts.

4. All drivers must be on time to compete in the events for which they are scheduled. When the first car is on the starting line, a limit of five minutes may be set in which other drivers should line up. Any driver or car not ready to compete when called may be sent to the rear of the line in time trials or races; changed to a later race; or left out of the remainder of the day's racing at the discretion of the NASCAR Official in charge of the event.

5. Once the field is lined up and the starter signals the drivers to be ready, a limit of three preliminary laps may be set at the discretion of the starter, who will then start the race. Disposition of cars not in position shall be at the discretion of officials. This rule as well as Number 4 shall apply on restarts also. Race begins at commencement of Pace Laps, but scoring and official distance begins when starting flag is displayed.

6. A race may be stopped at the discretion of the starter or officials at any time they consider it dangerous or unsafe to continue.

7. Except in Grand National, Western Grand National, Grand American and Late Model Sportsman and Modified National Championship races, when a race is stopped before the completion of one lap there shall be a complete restart in the original starting positions EXCEPT that cars involved in an accident, if any, shall start in the rear of others.

   a. Any cars causing a race to be stopped, such as a spinout, shall be considered as involved in an accident.

   b. Any cars stopping due to a mishap and not driven immediately

---

to the starting line shall be considered as involved in an accident.

NOTE: Interpretation of the words "Spinout" in paragraph 7a and "immediately" in paragraph 7b shall be left to the judgment of the Chief Steward and his decision shall be final.

8. In Grand National, Western Grand National, Grand American and Late Model Sportsman and Modified National Championship races, if a race is stopped before the completion of one lap, cars will restart in their original starting positions.

9. When a race is stopped after the completion of one lap, cars shall line up in the order in which they were running at the completion of the last full lap before being stopped. Those cars involved in the accident, if any, shall start in the rear of those not involved. Regardless of the number of laps they have covered, this rule shall apply at all times and in the event that enough laps have been covered for the race to be called a complete event, drivers will be scored and paid on the positions they would have held in a restart.

   NOTE: Rules 7, 8 and 9 supersede any track or ground rules.

10. All races shall be run until the leader covers the advertised distance. In the event unforeseen circumstances prevent the completion of the advertised distance, the race will be considered officially completed after the halfway mark has been reached provided circumstances make it impossible to continue the race within a reasonable time after it has been stopped.

   a. Lap time penalties must be executed by bringing violator to pits immediately and imposing penalty. No driver shall receive a lap or time penalty after the completion of a race.

FINISH LINE INTERPRETATION — On tracks that have recessed pit areas, the finish line shall be considered to extend from the grandstand retaining wall to the work pit wall, and any car rolling through the pits under his own power may legally receive the white flag or the checkered flag.

11. The ranking NASCAR official assigned to an event will have the responsibility of determining if the race track or speedway is in raceable condition for that event.

12. Except as otherwise provided in Sanction Agreement or official Entry Blanks published for the racemeet, when a racemeet is halted due to rain or a curfew the promoter must refund money and/or issue rainchecks, prize money shall be paid only to winning drivers in those events completed.

13. Except as otherwise provided in Sanction Agreement or official Entry Blanks published for the racemeet, when a racemeet is halted due to rain or other adverse circumstances and the promoter does not issue rainchecks, those races not completed, and the prize money for same, shall be carried over as part of a double feature

racemeet on the next scheduled race date at the same track. The program shall start with the incomplete portion of the previous racemeet and all original entries shall start in the position they held when the race was stopped. Qualifying positions previously earned shall apply. Tracks operating more than once a week shall have the right to designate the date for the completion of the rained out events.

14. No race shall be considered official until the official declaration of winning positions is made by the NASCAR official in charge of the event or events.

15. When time trials are held on days prior to date of racemeet, NASCAR reserves the right to seal all motors or impound cars.

16. All participants are subject to NASCAR rules and regulations when on the racing premises; and when cars get underway on a pace lap it shall be considered the start of an event.

17. No car may be pushed past the flagman at the end of the pit road. After race is underway, cars may be started by hand pushing in pit area only, but under no circumstances is any car to be pushed or towed onto race track from pit area. Violation means disqualification. No car may receive any assistance after white flag has been displayed, except cars making regular pit stops.

18. When a car runs over the air hose during pit stop, car will be held up for a one lap penalty. When the car runs over the jack, car must return to assigned pit for the crew to inspect tires. Penalties will only be invoked on the observation of a penalty by a NASCAR official.

19. All cars must be on the race track ready to go when the pace lap starts, and under no circumstances is any car not in the starting line-up to go on the track or enter the race after the completion of the green flag lap.

20. A pit crew member stopping a car during a pit stop is not permitted to have any tools to service the car.

21. All major car repairs must be performed behind the pit wall.

22. No car will be permitted on the race track at any time unless the gas tank cap remains in closed position on the filler spout. Any car observed without gas tank cap in closed position on the filler spout may be flagged into the pits and kept in the pits until the gas tank cap is placed in its proper position.

SECTION 10 — SPECIAL RULES

1. Special rules may be made by NASCAR official in charge for a certain area, track or racemeet due to extraordinary conditions, and must be made known to all competitors before racemeet or event by means of a bulletin, Newsletter, telegram, entry blank or pre-race meeting.

2. Special rules issued from NASCAR Headquarters will be

considered as official amendments to the 1971 NASCAR rules, regulations and specifications.

3. Special rules in regard to specifications for weekly events will not be in effect for any NASCAR racing division until such rules or changes are issued by NASCAR Headquarters in bulletin form. NASCAR Newsletters will be considered as official bulletins.

SECTION 11 — PERFORMANCE TRIALS

1. Conditions governing all safety and/or performance trials to be operated under NASCAR sanction and for which certificates of performance are to be issued shall be established and approved by the NASCAR Technical Committee and shall be approved by the National Stock Car Racing Commission.

SECTION 12 — SPECIAL TESTS

1. Special tests of any kind may be run under NASCAR supervision.
2. Conditions for all special tests shall be approved by the National Stock Car Racing Commission.

SECTION 13 — FLAG RULES

Any driver who does not obey the flag rules will be subject to disqualification and fine. Where light signals are also used, definite understanding concerning these signals in relation to the flags shall be made before the race.

GREEN FLAG — Start of race.
BLUE FLAG WITH YELLOW STRIPE OR MARKER — For passing and will be displayed only to cars that are being lapped.
YELLOW FLAG — Caution, go slow, single file, hold position — NO PASSING.
RED FLAG — Danger, race stops immediately.
BLACK FLAG — Pull off track for consultation.
WHITE FLAG — One lap to go.
CHECKERED FLAG — End of race.

GREEN FLAG

1. When the green flag is given by the starter, cars must retain position until they have crossed the starting line. The NASCAR official in charge of the event may make special ruling on restarts. On restarts, the race will resume immediately when the green flag is displayed.

2. In all races, each car must remain in assigned starting position until the starting line has been crossed, and the No. 2 qualifier must not beat the No. 1 qualifier to the green flag.
PENALTY FOR VIOLATION — Violators will be black flagged.

YELLOW FLAG

1. The yellow flag signifies caution and this flag will be given to the first car passing the starter. After the yellow flag is displayed,

cars must hold position until either the green flag is again displayed, or the red flag which would automatically stop the race.

2. Cars must slow down to a cautious pace on all yellow flags.

3. In the event a caution car is used, no car unless directed to do so by an official in the caution car, may pass the caution car, and any cars illegally passing the caution car shall be black flagged. The starter will signify one lap before the green flag will again be displayed. All cars must stay in single file until the green flag is displayed.

(a) When Caution Car is used the NASCAR official in charge of the event will designate the driver of the caution car.

4. While the yellow flag is being displayed, no member of pit crews will be allowed to cross the pit border line onto the race course to contact car or driver. Violation will mean loss of one lap.

a. Pit attendants and mechanics must not go on the race track to give the driver water, or for any other reason, while the cars are racing, or while they are running under the yellow flag. The only time drivers or cars may receive service is when they are completely stopped, in the pits.

5. Cars returning to the race course from the pits while the yellow flag is out must wait for rear end of the field in line behind the caution car, or as directed by the pit flagman.

6. No pit crews may service or repair any wrecked or damaged car until the car has been removed from race course.

RED FLAG

The red flag means that the race must be stopped immediately regardless of position of cars on track. The red flag shall be used if, in the opinion of starter, the track is unsafe to continue race. Cars should be brought to starting line if possible and kept on track proper. No repairs of any nature or refueling will be permitted when the race is halted due to a red flag. All work must stop on any car in the pits when red flag is displayed, and work cannot be resumed until race is restarted. Any driver not obeying red flag signal shall be subject to disqualification, fine and/or suspension.

BLACK FLAG

1. Black flag means go to pits immediately — report to NASCAR official at your pit. Does not mean automatic disqualification. However, failure to obey black flag will result in disqualification, suspension and/or fine.

2. In all races, if the hood or rear deck lid comes open, the starter must show said car the black flag as soon as possible, and any driver attempting to continue in competition with the hood open will be immediately disqualified.

NOTE: When black and red flags are displayed together, it signals the end of practice — clear the track.

WHITE FLAG

1. When the white flag is displayed it means you have started into your last lap.

2. No car may receive any assistance after said car has received the white flag, except cars on a regular pit stop.

CHECKERED FLAG

1. When checkered flag is displayed it means race is finished. When the required race distance has been completed by the lead car, the race will be declared "official" regardless of what flag has been displayed. (Final disposition of any flag dispute will be decided by NASCAR official in charge of the event).

2. When the checkered flag is given the leader, the balance of the field receives the checkered flag in the same lap. Finishing positions will be paid off according to most laps traveled in the least time, regardless of whether the car is still running or not.

3. The driver receiving the checkered flag first in any feature race must bring his car to the starting line and remain there until released by the NASCAR official in charge of the event.

SPECIAL FLAGS

(Including passing flag). Special flags may be used at the discretion of starter and officials, but must be fully explained to all contestants before the races start.

SECTION 14 — VIOLATIONS

1. All members of NASCAR are subject to disciplinary action for violation of these rules.

2. Penalties for violation of these rules include disqualification, suspension, fine or loss of points. The nature of the penalty is determined by the gravity of the offense and its effect on the safety and good reputation of stock car automobile racing.

a. Unless otherwise specified on the Penalty Notice, all unpaid fines shall be deducted at the end of the season from any point fund money earned by the member to whom the Penalty Notice has been issued. (Any fines left unpaid at the end of a racing season will be considered as grounds for automatic indefinite suspension).

3. The violations hereinafter set forth are subject to the penalties noted:

a. Any member who fails to sign all releases and required forms when signing in at race track Registration Office may be disqualified and any prize money or points won in the race may be forfeited.

b. Any driver, car owner or mechanic who permits a car to be driven in any NASCAR racemeet by an unlicensed person, or who fails to notify NASCAR officials of any change of driver during a racemeet, shall be fined or suspended.

c. Any member who assaults or threatens to do bodily harm to any NASCAR official or persons serving under his direction shall be suspended, fine not to exceed $500.00, and lose all accumulated points.

d. Any NASCAR member who participates in fights in pits, track or race premises shall be fined a minimum of $100.00 and may also be suspended.

e. Any member who, while participating in a NASCAR sanctioned event, partakes of any alcoholic beverage, stimulating or tranquilizing drug shall be immediately ejected from the racing premises and shall be subject to mandatory fine of not less than $25.00 and not more than $500.00 and suspension.

f. Any member who fails to obtain a competitor permit and sign the release sheet for that particular meet will be subject to a mandatory fine of $25 and/or disqualification of driver and car associated with the violation.

g. Any member who permits someone else to use his competitor permit will be subject to a mandatory fine of $25 and/or disqualification.

h. Any member who permits someone else to use his license will be subject to a mandatory fine of $25 and suspension. Any member who uses a license other than his own is also subject to fine and suspension.

i. Any member who signs the NASCAR release sheet or competitor permit for anyone other than himself shall be subject to a minimum fine of $25.00.

j. Any driver who competes in a car he is not eligible to drive shall forfeit all prize money and points won in the race, and may forfeit all championship points won in pervious race meets, and shall be subject to a fine and/or suspension.

k. Except for Grand National, Western Grand National, Grand American or any other events for which Official entry blanks are published by NASCAR Headquarters, any NASCAR member, licensed as a driver or car owner, who files an entry or in any way commits himself to participate in such an event and fails to do so without seeking and receiving the consent of the NASCAR Competition Director at least 24 hours before the event, shall be subject to any one or more of the following penalties for each such failure to participate, whether or not he takes part in another motor sports event on the same day: (a) a minimum charge of $25.00, (b) loss of all NASCAR championship points for the year in which the failure to participate occurs, or (c) indefinite suspension.

(1) In Grand National, Western Grand National, Grand American or any other events for which Official entry blanks are published by NASCAR Headquarters, any NASCAR member, licensed as a driver or car owner, who files an entry or in any way commits himself to participate in such an event and fails to do so without seeking and receiving the consent of the NASCAR Competition Director at least 24 hours before the event, shall be subject to any one or more of the following penalties for each such failure to participate, if he does not take part in another motor sports event on the same day: (a) a minimum charge of $50.00, (b) loss of all NASCAR championship points for the year in which the failure to participate occurs, or (c) indefinite suspension; however, if said driver or car owner fails to participate as heretofore described and takes part in another motor sports event on the same day, he may be subject to any one or more of the following penalties: (a) a minimum charge of $200.00, (b) loss of all NASCAR championship points for the year in which the failure to participate occurs, or (c) indefinite suspension.

l. Any promoter or track operator who fails to fulfill his agreement with NASCAR in connection with any sanctioned racemeet may be denied further sanctions at any track until all obligations have been discharged.

m. At all official inspections, any automotive parts which are found not to comply with NASCAR rules and specifications shall be impounded and forwarded to NASCAR Headquarters. Should the driver, owner or mechanic refuse to surrender the part or parts involved, he is subject to automatic disqualification. For such disqualification, the car owner and driver forfeit all the prize money and points for the event. A second disqualification in any one year subjects the car owner and driver to an additional penalty of loss of all points earned to date plus a minimum fine of $200.00, and a fifteen day license suspension. A third disqualification in any year subjects the car owner and driver, to indefinite suspension of license.

n. Any member, licensed as a driver or car owner, who permits his car to be taken from the racing area after the finish of an event without first obtaining permission from the NASCAR official in charge of the event is subject to disqualification. For such disqualification, the owner and driver forfeit all points for the event as well as the prize money.

o. Any entrant who performs an act or participates in actions deemed by NASCAR Officials as detrimental to the sport or to NASCAR, or fails to abide by the provisions set forth in the entry blank, shall be subject to loss of all NASCAR championship points.

SECTION 15 — PROTESTS AND ADJUDICATION

1. For a rule violation which the NASCAR official in charge of the event determines involves the safety of participants or spectators, the said official is authorized to summarily disqualify, fine, suspend or eject the violator from the racing premises. The use of intoxicants or drugs, fighting and reckless driving are examples of violations included under this rule.

2. All rule violations for which summary action is not taken by the NASCAR official in charge of the event shall be reported in writing and in detail, to Lin Kuchler, Competition Director, at NASCAR Headquarters for adjudication.

3. Any NASCAR member against whom disciplinary action has been instituted shall have the right to a protest hearing at NASCAR Headquarters, or wherever else NASCAR may designate, if such member shall mail such request for a hearing to NASCAR Headquarters within not more than 10 days from date of the written notice of said disciplinary action issued by the Competition Director, along with a $100.00 protest fee. In any such hearing, a member shall have the right to appear in his own behalf, and to present witnesses and documentary evidence.

4. Any affected member may, as a matter of right, protest any violation of these rules, specifications or entry blank terms to the Competition Director in accordance with the following procedure:

a. A protest shall be brought to the attention of the NASCAR official in charge of the event as soon as the alleged violation is discovered by the protestant and must be filed in writing with said official not later than fifteen minutes after completion of the event in which the alleged violation occurred. Each separate protest shall be accompanied by $100.00 protest fee.

b. If the parties to the protest do not accept the said NASCAR official's decision on the protest, it shall be forwarded with the protest fee to the Competition Director at NASCAR Headquarters.

c. All visual protests shall be made prior to start of feature event. All visual protests made after start of feature event will be void. (A visual protest is a protest which does not require any type of a measuring device to establish the legality of any part of an automobile.)

d. In race meets where pre-race technical inspections are conducted, no technical protests will be accepted later than 24 hours prior to scheduled start of race. NASCAR officials may call for a car inspection at any time.

e. Protests arising, other than out of a particular racing event, shall be filed in writing at NASCAR Headquarters with protest fee.

f. Protests involving local track or ground rules shall be determined by NASCAR officials at the track and are not appealable to the Competition Director, the National Stock Car Racing Commission or the Commissioner.

5. If the Competition Director sustains the protest, the protest fee shall be returned to the protesting member and the losing member shall pay all costs incurred by NASCAR officials in determining the protest. If the protest is not sustained, the $100.00 protest fee shall be forfeited, and the protesting member shall pay all costs incurred by NASCAR officials in determining the protest. When the protest is not sustained, the member against whom the protest is made shall be entitled to compensation not exceeding the amount of the protest fee for any preparation he is required to make for the purpose of determining the outcome of the protest, and such compensation shall be paid from the protest fee by NASCAR.

6. All disciplinary action will be announced at NASCAR Headquarters and the members involved will be notified in person or by mail addressed to their last recorded address.

7. NASCAR members against whom disciplinary action has been announced by NASCAR Headquarters shall have a right of appeal to the National Stock Car Racing Commission, as provided in Section 16 of these Rules, provided written notice of appeal together with the $100.00 appeal fee is furnished to the Commission within 30 days of the announcement by NASCAR Headquarters of the disciplinary action.

SECTION 16

NATIONAL STOCK CAR
RACING COMMISSION APPEALS

1. National Stock Car Racing Commission is established to rule on appeals. The Commission shall consist of 13 members.
Members of the Commission for 1971 are:

Russ Moyer — Chairman   Phil Holmer

Art Atkinson	Pete Keller
Bill Amick	Carleton Merrill
Bob Barkhimer	Ralph Ouderkirk
John Bruner, Sr.	Ken Piper
Bill Gazaway	Les Richter

Bob Sall

The Chairman of the Commission shall be the administrative member. In the event of death, retirement or inability of the Chairman to perform his duties, the member longest in continuous service shall perform the duties during the disability or until a successor member is elected.

The Commission shall hold an organizational meeting in February of each year which shall be called by the Chairman.

The Commission shall meet at such places and at such times as are necessary for the efficient and speedy disposition of its business. Three members constitute a quorum, except for the organizational meeting when seven members shall constitute a quorum.

In conducting a hearing the Commission shall not be bound by technical or formal rules of procedure except as provided herein, but shall conduct hearings in such manner as to best ascertain the rights of all parties to the proceedings under these rules.

The Commission may enact its own rules for the conduct of hearings, and the prescribed manner in which appeals may be decided. All appeals shall be docketed when received at National Headquarters and shall be set for hearing in the order same are docketed.

In the event a Commission member is involved in an appeal, the Commission member shall disqualify himself from participating as a Commission member on the appeal and the remaining Commission members shall select a replacement.

A majority of the members of the Commission present must concur to modify any penalty or determine any appeal. If the Commission fails to agree on action to be taken on an appeal, the appeal shall be referred to the NASCAR National Stock Car Racing Commissioner for decision.

Members may appear in person at hearings before the Commission. All testimony before the Commission shall be under oath. When testimony is taken, the testimony shall upon motion of either party or the order of the Commission, be taken down in writing and filed in the proceedings.

2. In each appeal the relevant item shall be the correctness of the ruling by the NASCAR official involved in light of the facts and not the results of the ruling.

3. If the Commission determines that the proceedings in respect to any appeal have been instituted or continued without reasonable grounds, the cost of such proceedings shall be assessed against the member who instituted or continued such proceedings.

SECTION 16A—NATIONAL COMMISSIONER

An office for the National Stock Car Racing Commissioner shall be maintained at NASCAR National Headquarters, Daytona Beach, Fla., and a fund will be maintained for the operation of this office.

The National Stock Car Racing Commissioner will serve for $1 per year.

The National Stock Car Racing Commissioner shall be nominated and appointed as follows: The NASCAR President will name a committee of three to select a candidate for appointment and the action ... subject to the ratification of at least 10

promoters of NASCAR sanctioned events. Members of the nominating committee will consist of one NASCAR official and two promoters of NASCAR sanctioned events.

The office of National Stock Car Racing Commissioner is established to provide a supreme authority for the administration of orderly procedures in automotive events and the enforcement of the provisions of the Rule Book.

The Commissioner shall be the final appellate authority with regard to a violation of these rules, specifications, entry blank terms, or disciplinary procedures, and any affected member may as a matter of right appeal any decision of the National Stock Car Racing Commission in accordance with the following procedure:

a. An appeal shall be in writing and filed with Russ Moyer, Chairman, National Stock Car Racing Commission, at National Headquarters within 20 days of the decision of the Commission together with a $100.00 appeal fee.

b. The Commissioner shall conduct a hearing on the appeal at the earliest practicable date, notifying the parties of said appeal and hearing. Date and place of hearing shall be determined by the National Stock Car Racing Commissioner.

c. Members may appear in person at hearings before the Commissioner. All testimony before the Commissioner shall be taken under oath. When testimony is taken, the testimony shall, upon motion of either party or by order of the Commissioner, be taken down in writing and filed with the proceedings.

d. Hearings before the Commissioner shall be conducted under the rules promulgated by the Commissioner.

e. All decisions of the Commissioner shall be final.

f. If the Commissioner determines that the proceedings in respect to any appeal have been continued by a protesting member without reasonable grounds, the cost of such proceedings shall be assessed against the protesting member who continued the proceedings.

SECTION 17 — PRIZE MONEY

1. All NASCAR races shall be contested for a guaranteed finishing position purse as per the entry blank or the pay-off schedule.

2. Prize money shall be based on track size, location, seating capacity, attendance and type of racemeet.

3. NASCAR members agree to abide by decisions of NASCAR officers in establishing amount of prize money for each track.

4. Prize money in all race competitions shall be payable to the driver, and each driver will be solely responsible for the settlement

with his car owner. Prize money shall be distributed by the NASCAR officials assigned to the event.

5. All undistributed prize money shall be forwarded to NASCAR Headquarters for distribution.

6. NASCAR competitors are entitled to see entry blank, program of events and prize money distribution before any racemeet or contest.

7. NASCAR members who compete in racemeet or contest are entitled to inspect completed copy of official pay-off for racemeet.

8. In the event of protest, prize money involved shall be forwarded to NASCAR Headquarters for decision, accompanied by written statements from those involved. After a decision has been reached, prize money will be forwarded from NASCAR Headquarters along with written copies of decision. NASCAR expenses incurred in settling any such protest will be deducted from the prize money of those requesting the NASCAR Headquarters' re-check of the scorer's decision.

9. Promoter may not revise purse downward without previous notice and approval of the Chief Steward. When races are held on regular schedule, such as weekly or twice weekly, all contestants must be notified of any downward revision of prize money not later than pay-off time of previous racemeet.

SECTION 18 — POINT FUNDS

1. Point fund money must be paid for all race meets according to the schedules shown in 4a and 4b of this section.

a. Points and point fund money will be established on a national basis for the Grand National, Western Grand National and Grand American divisions, and points will be awarded according to schedules shown in sub-paragraph 5a and distributed to drivers and car owners according to schedules shown in sub-paragraphs 6a and 6b.

b. Points and point fund money will be established on national, state and track basis for Late Model Sportsman and Modified divisions, and on state and track basis for Hobby division. Points will be awarded according to schedule shown in sub-paragraph 5c and distributed to drivers only according to schedule shown in sub-paragraph 6c.

(1) In events designated as Late Model Sportsman or Modified National, State or Sectional Championships, points and point fund money will be established on a national

basis and awarded according to the schedule shown in sub-paragraph 5b and distributed to drivers only according to the schedule shown in sub-paragraph 6e. A race must carry a $4,000 minimum purse to qualify as a National, State or Sectional Championship.

NOTE: Tracks operating on a weekly basis will be allowed two non-championship races per season for which double points will be awarded upon approval from NASCAR. One double point program may be awarded on the completion of five regular programs. (NO DOUBLE POINTS AWARDED FOR NATIONAL, STATE OR SECTIONAL CHAMPIONSHIP RACES).

2. A driver will be credited only with points earned in the car in which he started the feature or championship event, and the driver starting the car will be credited with all points earned by that car in that event. A driver cannot receive points for more than one car in any race.

NOTE: It is customary for drivers to share their point money with their car owners, and should the drivers be called upon to name the owners of the cars in which they accumulated the greatest number of points, they alone will be responsible for the selections.

3. In case of any ties, monies and points for the tied positions shall be pooled and divided equally among the contestants involved.

4. **POINT FUNDS WILL BE ESTABLISHED AS FOLLOWS: (In no division will manufacturers' prize money be considered in the establishment of the point fund).**

a. Grand National, Western Grand National, and Grand American divisions.
(1) Events up to 249 miles—$75 per thousand of purse payoff.
(2) Events 250 to 399 miles—$100 per thousand of purse payoff.
(3) Events 400 miles and over—$125 per thousand of purse payoff.

b. All other divisions (regardless of race distances): $5 per hundred of purse payoff.

NOTE: Point fund money will be apportioned as follows in these divisions:
(1) Late Model Sportsman division: 75 per cent to track fund, 10 per cent to state fund, 15 per cent to national fund.
(2) Modified division: 75 per cent to track fund, 10 per cent to state fund, 15 per cent to national fund.
(3) Hobby division, (which includes Late Model Hobby and Cadet class, and Limited Sportsman): 75 per cent to track fund, 25 per cent to state fund.

5. CHAMPIONSHIP POINTS WILL BE AWARDED AS FOLLOWS:

a. Grand National, Western Grand National and Grand American divisions. (Points will be awarded for finishing position only).

Events to 249 Miles
50 points to win, with one point less for each succeeding position.
50, 49, 48, 47, etc.

Events 250 to 399 Miles
100 points to win, with two points less for each succeeding position.
100, 98, 96, 94, etc.

Events 400 Miles & over
150 points to win, with three points less for each succeeding position.
150, 147, 144, 141, etc.

b. Late Model Sportsman and Modified National, State or Sectional championship races (Points awarded according to amounts of posted purses as follows):

Pos.	$4,000	$5,000	$6,000	$7,000	$8,000	$9,000	$10,000	$25,000
1.	200	250	300	350	400	450	500	1,250
2.	192	240	288	336	384	432	480	1,200
3.	184	230	276	322	368	414	460	1,150
4.	176	220	264	308	352	396	440	1,100
5.	168	210	252	294	336	378	420	1,050
6.	160	200	240	280	320	360	400	1,000
7.	152	190	228	266	304	342	380	950
8.	144	180	216	252	288	324	360	900
9.	136	170	204	238	272	306	340	850
10.	128	160	192	224	256	288	320	800
11.	120	150	180	210	240	270	300	750
12.	112	140	168	196	224	252	280	700
13.	104	130	156	182	208	234	260	650
14.	96	120	144	168	192	216	240	600
15.	88	110	132	154	176	198	220	550
16.	80	100	120	140	160	180	200	500
17.	72	90	108	126	144	162	180	450
18.	64	80	96	112	128	144	160	400
19.	56	70	84	98	112	126	140	350
20.	48	60	72	84	96	108	120	300
21.	40	50	60	70	80	90	100	250
22.	32	40	48	56	64	72	80	200
23.	24	30	36	42	48	54	60	150
24.	16	20	24	28	32	36	40	100
25.	8	10	12	14	16	18	20	50

All Starters Receive Minimum as Per Schedule.

(National, State or Sectional Championship Races not eligible for double points)

c. All other divisions, including Late Model Sportsman and Modified

---

according to finishing positions as follows:

Pos.	Pts.	Pos.	Pts.	Pos.	Pts.
1	50	9	34	18	16
2	48	10	32	19	14
3	46	11	30	20	12
4	44	12	28	21	10
5	42	13	26	22	8
6	40	14	24	23	6
7	38	15	22	24	4
8	36	16	20	25	2
		17	18		

(All finishers below 25th position receive 2 points each)

6. POINT FUNDS WILL BE DISTRIBUTED AS FOLLOWS:

a. Grand National drivers:
After the point fund in this division has been divided one-half to the drivers' fund and one-half to the car owners' fund, distribution of the point fund money to drivers will be made according to the following percentage schedule:

Place	% of Total	Place	% of Total
1st	20	11th	3
2nd	10	12th	3
3rd	9	13th	3
4th	8	14th	3
5th	7	15th	3
6th	6	16th	2
7th	5	17th	2
8th	4	18th	2
9th	3	19th	2
10th	3	20th	2

b. Grand American and Western Grand National drivers:
After the point funds in these divisions have been divided two-thirds to the drivers' fund and one-third to the car owners' fund, distribution of the point fund money to drivers will be made according to the following percentage schedule:

Place	% of Total	Place	% of Total
1st	20	11th	3
2nd	10	12th	3
3rd	9	13th	3
4th	8	14th	3
5th	7	15th	3
6th	6	16th	2
7th	5	17th	2
8th	4	18th	2
9th	3	19th	2
10th	2	20th	2

ing percentage schedule:

Place	% of Total	Place	% of Total
1st	20	11th	3
2nd	10	12th	3
3rd	9	13th	3
4th	8	14th	3
5th	7	15th	3
6th	6	16th	2
7th	5	17th	2
8th	4	18th	2
9th	3	19th	2
10th	3	20th	2

7. Grand National Manufacturer's Point Fund Championship.

Points to be awarded to a car division (Dodge, Plymouth, Ford, Mercury, etc.) for the top six finishing positions in each Grand National race, distributed as follows:

Pos.	Pts.	Pos.	Pts.
1	9	4	3
2	6	5	2
3	4	6	1

A manufacturer will be eligible for points for the best position only. (Example: If a Ford finishes in the top three positions and a Chevrolet finishes in fourth position, Ford will receive 9 points and Chevrolet will receive 3 points. No points will be awarded for second and third positions). To be eligible for points, a car must finish in the top six positions.

8. NASCAR reserves the right to establish, maintain, compile, publish and otherwise operate and award points and point funds and trophies through the facilities of the Awards and Achievement Bureau of NASCAR, Inc., under its rules and regulations.

a. All members agree to abide by decisions of NASCAR officers in establishing and administering the point funds.

9. The 1971 championship point season for the Grand National division and Grand American series will officially close December 31, 1971. The 1971 championship point season for all other divisions will officially close on November 7, 1971, and any races scheduled thereafter shall count toward the 1972 standings.

10. All point money will be awarded at the annual Victory Awards dinner with date and place to be announced at the conclusion of the season.

a. Eligibility to participate in the point fund may be forfeited by any member violating NASCAR rules and/or regulations prior to the presentation of the 1971 awards at the Awards and Victory dinner in 1972.

... in paragraphs 6a and 6b will be determined on the basis of the number of points a driver has accumulated after his race position points (paragraph 5a) are multiplied by the number of races in which he receives a race multiple. One car multiple will be awarded for each race in which the driver has made a bonafide effort to compete, provided he has submitted a signed entry blank for the race before the official closing date for entries shown on the entry blank.

EXAMPLE:

Race Position Points		Number of Races		Points to be used For Point Fund Dist.
3,364	x	47	=	158,108

NOTE: Race multiples are used only to determine the number of points on which a driver's point fund distribution is predicated, and will not affect the Official Driver Point standing.

c. Grand National car owners:
Race multiples will not be used in determining the car owner point fund distribution in this division which will be made according to the following percentage schedule:

Place	% of Total	Place	% of Total
1st	20	11th	3
2nd	10	12th	3
3rd	9	13th	3
4th	8	14th	3
5th	7	15th	3
6th	6	16th	2
7th	5	17th	2
8th	4	18th	2
9th	3	19th	2
10th	3	20th	2

d. Grand American and Western Grand National car owners:
Race multiples will not be used in determining the car owner point fund distribution in these divisions which will be made according to the following percentage schedule:

Place	% of Total	Place	% of Total
1st	25	6th	7
2nd	15	7th	6
3rd	12	8th	5
4th	11	9th	5
5th	10	10th	4

e. All other divisions (Driver points only. No car owner points in these divisions):
Race multiples will not be used in determining driver point fund distribution which will be made according to the follow-

11. In the event the championship point fund collected at any track for any division does not exceed $200 at the end of the season, the portion usually assigned for track distribution will be transferred to the State, National or trophy funds as the case may be, and a track champion will not be named. In the event a track fails to run the required 10 events necessary for an official championship, the division of the point money will follow the same formula.

SECTION 19

FEDERATION INTERNATIONALE de l'AUTOMOBILE

The Federation Internationale de l'Automobile, hereinafter referred to as the "FIA", is the sole international authority entitled to make and enforce rules and regulations for the encouragement and control of automobile competitions (including records), and is the final international court of appeal for the settlement of disputes arising therefrom.

The FIA has established an International Sporting Code, hereinafter called the "Code", which provides (among other things):

That each Sporting Authority (ASN belonging to the FIA) shall accept and be bound by the Code.

That the National Sporting Authority, subject to such acceptance, shall be recognized by the FIA as the sole body having power to control automobile competitions in its own country, territories and protectorates.

That a National Sporting Authority shall have the right to delegate the whole or part of the powers granted by the Code to one or more Clubs in its country, provided the consent of the FIA is first obtained, and to revoke such delegation if it notifies the FIA.

That a National Sporting Authority may draw up its own National Competition Rules, but such Rules must be in conformity with the Code and approved by the FIA. Pending approval by the FIA, the Rules may be provisionally enforced.

The Automobile Competition Committee for the United States-FIA is recognized by the FIA as the National Sporting Authority (ASN) of the U.S.A., and is generally referred to as ACCUS-FIA. NASCAR, USAC, SCCA and NHRA are members of ACCUS.

ACN (Automobile Club National) has been replaced by ASN (Autorite Sportive Nationale).

Automobiles meeting NASCAR Grand National Division specifications are referred to as Stock Cars.

Competitors holding FIA licenses may be recognized in world-wide competition and may be privileged to compete in many events listed on the FIA International calendar.

SECTION 20

NASCAR GRAND NATIONAL CHAMPIONSHIP DIVISION
INCLUDING
WESTERN GRAND NATIONAL DIVISION

America's greatest auto race drivers competing with the finest equipment developed by America's automotive manufacturers.

1. COMPETING MODELS

a. NASCAR Grand National races are open to steel bodied 1969, 1970, 1971 models of American-made passenger car production sedans, available to the general public, classified as follows: Standard and Intermediate.

The specifications for the Grand National Division, in essentially the same form as listed here, have been accepted by the Automobile Competition Club of the United States — FIA and by the FIA for inclusion in the Appendix J. They will be listed in Category 5B of the special touring sedan section.

Category 1—Standard size cars.

Limited to cars with a minimum of 119-inch wheelbase, a maximum engine size of 430 cubic inches piston displacement, standard body size and complying with minimum weight requirement as set forth in paragraph 1b. (OVERBORING: A total maximum of one cubic inch will be permitted for overboring because of cylinder wear).

The following 1971 cars have been classified in Category 1 —

AMERICAN MOTORS—Ambassador
BUICK—Riviera, Riviera Grand-
sport, Electra 225, Electra
Custom Sport Coupe, Cen-
turion, LeSabre, LeSabre Sport
Coupe, LeSabre Custom Sport
Coupe
CHEVROLET—Caprice, Impala
CHRYSLER—Newport, Newport
Custom, 300, New Yorker,
Imperial
DODGE—Polara, Monaco
FORD—Galaxie 500, LTD
MERCURY—Marquis, Monterey
OLDSMOBILE—Delta 88, 98, Royale
88, Toronado, Custom 88
PLYMOUTH—Fury I, Fury II,
Fury III, Sport Fury, Fury GT
PONTIAC—Catalina, Bonneville,
Grandville

The following 1970 cars have been classified in Category 1 —

AMERICAN MOTORS—Ambassador
BUICK—LeSabre, Wildcat, Electra
225, Riviera
CADILLAC—Eldorado, 60 Special,
75 Limousine, Calais de Ville
CHEVROLET—Impala, Caprice,
Bel Air
CHRYSLER—Newport, 300, New
Yorker, Imperial
DODGE—Polara, Monaco
FORD—Galaxie, Custom
MERCURY—Marauder, Marquis,
Monterey
OLDSMOBILE—Delta 88, 98,
Toronado
PLYMOUTH—Fury
PONTIAC—Catalina, Executive,
Bonneville

The following 1969 cars have been classified in Category 1 —

AMERICAN MOTORS—Ambassador
BUICK—LeSabre, Wildcat, Electra 225, Riviera
CADILLAC—Eldorado, 60 Special, 75 Limousine, Calais de Ville
CHEVROLET—Impala, Caprice, Bel Air
CHRYSLER—Newport, 300, New Yorker, Imperial
DODGE—Polara, Monaco
FORD—Galaxie, Custom
MERCURY—Marauder, Marquis, Monterey
OLDSMOBILE—Delta 88, 98, Toronado
PLYMOUTH—Fury
PONTIAC—Catalina, Executive, Bonneville

Category 2—Intermediate size cars.

Limited to cars with a minimum of 115-inch wheelbase, and less than 119-inch wheelbase, a maximum engine size of 430 cubic inches piston displacement, standard body size and complying with minimum weight requirement as set forth in paragraph 1b. (OVERBORING: A total maximum of one cubic inch will be permitted for overboring because of cylinder wear.)

The following 1971 cars have been classified in Category 2 —

AMERICAN MOTORS—Matador
BUICK—Grand Sport, Skylark
CHEVROLET—Chevelle, Monte Carlo, Malibu
DODGE—Charger, Charger Coupe, Charger 500, Charger S.E., Charger Super Bee, Charger R.T.
FORD—Torino, Torino Cobra, Torino G.T., Torino Broughman
MERCURY—Montego, Montego MX, Montego Brougham, Cyclone, Cyclone G.T.
OLDSMOBILE—F-85, Cutlass 442 Cutlass S Coupe
PLYMOUTH—GTX, Satellite, Road Runner.
PONTIAC—GTO, LeMans, LeMans Sport, T-37, Grand Prix

The following 1970 cars have been classified in Category 2 —

AMERICAN MOTORS—Rebel
BUICK—Special, Skylark, GS 350, GS 400
CHEVROLET—Chevelle, Monte Carlo
DODGE—Coronet, Charger
FORD—Torino
MERCURY—Montego, Cyclone
OLDSMOBILE—F-85, Cutlass 442.
PLYMOUTH—Belvedere GTX, Road Runner, Superbird
PONTIAC—Tempest, GTO, Grand Prix

The following 1969 cars have been classified in Category 2 —

AMERICAN MOTORS—Rebel
BUICK—Special, Skylark, GS 350, GS 400
CHEVROLET—Chevelle
DODGE—Coronet, Charger 500, Charger Daytona
FORD—Torino, Talladega
MERCURY—Montego, Cyclone Spoiler
OLDSMOBILE—F-85
PLYMOUTH—Satellite
PONTIAC—Tempest, GTO

Category 3—Compact or GA Cars. (Not eligible in this division)

Limited to cars with a wheelbase of less than 115 inches, with a maximum engine size of 335 cubic inches piston displacement.

Category 4—Sports cars. (Not eligible in this division)

Category 5—Grand American cars. (Not eligible in this division)

b. FIA category 1 and category 2 Standard approved bodies may run with 366 or 430 cubic inch displacement engine equipped with one four-barrel 1 11/16" carburetor.

(1) All FIA category 1 and category 2 cars, regardless of engine displacement, must weigh a minimum of 3,800 pounds ready to race (gasoline, oil, water, etc.) without driver.

(2) Cars with approved size engines (306 to 430 cu. in.) may be required to use a carburetor restrictor plate when furnished by NASCAR. ACCUS has approved a differentiation in the carburetor plate opening size for hemispherical versus wedge type engines, as defined by NASCAR.

(3) Any weight added to car must be located within body shell. Special cars including the Mercury Cyclone Spoiler, Ford Talladega, Dodge Daytona, Dodge Charger 500, and Plymouth Superbird shall be limited to a maximum engine size of 305 cubic inches and a minimum weight of 3,800 pounds equipped with one four-barrel 1 11/16 inch carburetor.

c. Eligibility.

(1) It is mandatory that a street version engine be produced by the manufacturer as a regular production option for installation and sale to the public in a regular product offering. The 1971 eligible bodies will be volume production models as selected and approved by the ACCUS. Engine production requirements will continue to be 500 engines installed in cars before approval to compete is granted, and in the case of engines reduced to 366 cu. in., 500 identical basic engines must be produced and installed in cars before approval to compete is granted.

(2) Production models and production engines introduced by January 15, 1971, will be classified eligible for competition in 1971. New models or engines introduced after January 15, 1971, will not be eligible for competition until April 15, 1971, if approved by ACCUS. Any equipment introduced after April 15 will not be eligible during 1971.

The following characteristics must be identical with the production engine upon which recognition of type has been granted:

CYLINDER BLOCK
Material
Number of Cylinders
Angle of Cylinders
Number of Main Bearings

39

Integral or separate Cylinder Sleeves
Location of Camshaft
Overall Configuration

CYLINDER HEAD
Material
Number of Valves per Cylinder
Type of Combustion Chamber
Location of Spark Plug
Orientation of Spark Plug
Arrangement of Valves
Type of Valve Actuation
Number of Intake Ports
Number of Exhaust Ports
Center Distances of Intake Ports
Center Distances of Exhaust Ports
Shape of In & Ex Ports at mating faces of manifolds
Angle of Port Face relative to mating face of Head to Block
Firing Order

GENERAL
All parts must originate from stock production castings and forgings which have been machined according to the normal machining schedule utilized for standard production parts. They may be subsequently refined, modified and improved by further machining or rework.

(3) The ACCUS car classification committee will determine if the eligibility requirements have been met.

(4) All eligible engines can be used in the standard size (Category 1) or the intermediate size (Category 2) cars.

(5) There will be no weight or displacement handicap on any car or engine in 1971.

(6) Maximum engine displacement for Category 1 and Category 2 cars is 430 cubic inches or 366 cubic inches, with a total maximum of one cubic inch permitted for overboring because of cylinder wear.

(7) All model, engine or equipment changes or modifications not governed by NASCAR rules Section 20 c (1), (2) and (3) must be submitted for consideration of approval, not less than 30 days prior to the date of intended usage in NASCAR competition. The applicant will be notified of approval or rejection no less than 15 days before the date of intended use. Any equipment which does not conform to the specifications or tolerances contained in the NASCAR Rule Book, will not be eligible for approval during 1971.

NO CHANGES FROM STANDARD PRODUCTION AUTOMOBILES OR COMPONENT PARTS WILL BE PERMITTED EXCEPT AS SPECIFIED IN FOLLOWING SPECIFICATIONS:

2. ENGINE
a. See Rule 1-C.

b. Engine may be located so #1 spark plug on short side of engine block is in line with the upper ball joint except on Monte Carlo Chevrolet. However, this is the maximum allowable backward position of engine. When using the small block engine — engine must mount in standard location.

c. Internal polishing, porting, altering and/or relieving of motor parts permitted.

d. Maximum two valves per cylinder.

e. Oversize oil pans and oil coolers are not to be used unless approved by NASCAR. Oil pans must have a minimum ground clearance as specified under inspection procedures.

f. Engine displacement may be increased by boring or stroking provided the total displacement does not exceed maximum size for specified class.

g. Cylinder blocks must be production with standard external measurements in all respects with the exception of the permissible overbore.

h. Pistons optional.

i. Cylinder head must be standard production. Internal changes permitted. A cylinder head is considered to be a "Standard Production" head if:

(1) It is the required cylinder head for a previously approved complete engine, said engine being available as an optional engine for a regular factory product offering.

(2) It does not change combustion chamber, type of valve action (Push Rod) or number of valves, used in the cylinder head assembly of the approved engine.

j. Crankshaft — Standard production design. Stroke may be increased or decreased. Balancing permitted.

k. Camshaft optional.

(1) Rocker arm supports must be standard production in design and size.

(2) Ball or roller bearing rocker arms not allowed unless standard on volume production engines.

(3) Solid or hydraulic valve lifters optional. Roller tappets not allowed unless standard on volume production engines.

(4) Camshaft must be driven the same as approved production engine. Gear drive not allowed unless approved standard production.

3. ENGINE MOUNTS
a. Motor mounts must be reinforced.

sition (See 2. b).

c. All motor mounts must be securely bolted.

4. CARBURETOR

a. Carburetor must be NASCAR approved. Approval of carburetor shall mean approval for all competitors and cost of carburetor shall be a factor of consideration for approval. No external alterations permitted.

(1) Rocker arm hemispherical combustion chamber engines restricted to one four-barred carburetor having 1 11/16" throttle bore.

(2) Overhead cam type engines restricted to one four-barrel carburetor having 1 11/16 inch throttle bore.

(3) Wedge type engines restricted to one four-barrel carburetor having 1 11/16 inch throttle bore.

(4) Engines with staggered valve design restricted to one four-barrel carburetor having 1 11/16 inch throttle bore.

(5) Intake manifold unrestricted within manufacturers line, readily available to participants. Materials optional.

b. Fuel injection or superchargers not permitted.

c. Jets may be any size.

d. Carburetor restrictor plate must be used when furnished by NASCAR. The 4150 and 4500 series carburetors may be used on any approved engine. Only approved carburetors with a 1 11/16" throttle bore opening are permitted.

(1) The 4150 carburetor is permitted to use a 3/8" spacer, with 1 11/16" holes, furnished by NASCAR, to provide carburetor butterfly clearance between the carburetor base and the NASCAR restrictor plate

(2) The 4500 carburetor is permitted to use only gaskets at the carburetor base.

(3) Only a maximum of three 1/8" thickness gaskets are permitted under any carburetor.

(4) Gaskets cannot be altered in any manner. Only approved carburetors with a 1 11/16" throttle base opening are permitted and the approved carburetor cannot be altered in any manner.

e. Heat risers may be blocked.

f. Any NASCAR approved gasoline filters may be used. This applies to all late model divisions as well as speed trial and record attempts.

5. ELECTRICAL

a. Ignition system must be standard for make and model. Automatic advance in distributor must be in complete working condition. Any make or brand of points may be used. NASCAR approved transistor systems may be used.

b. Any make or brand of spark plugs may be used. This applies

c. Batteries must remain under hood as near original standard location as possible and must be standard size for make and model. Alternate battery location must be approved.

d. The generator system must be working within specifications.

e. Self-starter must be in working order. All cars must start under their own power. After race is underway, cars may be started by hand pushing in pit area only, but under no circumstances is any car to be pushed or towed onto race track from pit area. Violation means disqualification.

6. COOLING SYSTEM

a. Water pump impellers may be altered.

b. Removal of fan blades, fan belt or air cleaner not permitted. Any NASCAR approved air cleaners allowed, and they must have the complete element. Only standard minimum four blade fan permitted. This applies to all late model divisions as well as speed trial and record attempts.

c. Interchangeable radiator cores are allowed providing they do not alter sheet metal or frame of radiator for make and model. Radiator must remain stock appearing and remain in standard position.

d. Radiator dust screens permitted.

e. Any brand or make of radiator hose or hose clamp permitted.

f. Radiator overflow pipe may be relocated or extended to not more than six feet.

7. LUBRICATION

a. Any oil is permissible.

b. Oil pressure may be regulated at discretion of owner or driver.

c. Any NASCAR approved oil filters and breather caps may be used. This applies to all late model divisions as well as speed trial and record attempts. Dry sump oiling system may be used, but must be NASCAR approved. During running of the race, oil must be added from the engine compartment. The reservoir capacity shall be limited to 1,155 cubic inches and location and installation must be NASCAR approved.

8. EXHAUST

a. Muffler must be removed, exhaust manifold optional. Pipes from muffler take-off must be no larger than four inches inside diameter when round exhaust pipe is used. Maximum one 4" pipe per side. Any other system must be approved by NASCAR. Exhaust pipes must extend past driver and to the outer edge of the car, beneath frame, with a minimum ground clearance of four inches. Exhaust pipes must come out on side of car in front of rear wheels only.

b. Extra brackets are mandatory.

c. The chief inspector reserves right to reject improperly mounted or unsafe exhaust pipes.

9. CLUTCH AND FLYWHEEL

a. High speed clutch assembly permitted as long as flywheel weight is not changed.

b. Size, weights and material must be normal customer production only.

c. A steel scattershield, not less than 3/8 inch thick, must be installed over flywheel and clutch area. Special construction all-steel clutch housings are permitted in lieu of separate scattershield. "Clutch-Flywheel Flexible Housing Safety Shield" is approved for use.

10. BELL HOUSING

a. No changes from normal production.

b. Starter mounting position must remain same as on standard production bell housing.

11. TRANSMISSIONS

a. Standard production, which are cataloged and available through regular dealer channels may be interchanged in any model.

b. All forward gears and reverse gear must be in working order.

12. DRIVE SHAFT

a. Drive shaft and universals must be similar in design to standard production type.

b. It is mandatory that two U-shaped brackets, no less than 2 inches wide and 1/4 inch thick, be placed around the drive shaft and fastened to the floor or cross member of car to prevent drive shaft from becoming dislodged and dropping to race track.

13. REAR AXLE

a. Rear axle ring and pinion may be any gear ratio.

b. Differentials optional. No quick change rear ends permitted.

c. Full floating rear axle compulsory, but must not alter tread width or general appearance. Limited slip differential permitted. When limited slip differential is used, one wheel, when jacked up, must turn freely by hand for one full turn—360°.

d. Differential oil coolers, approved by NASCAR, permitted.

14. FRAMES

a. Frames may be reinforced and altered for tire clearance and to permit the use of 9½ inch wheels, exhaust headers and shock absorbers. But the wheelbase must remain the same as manufactured as referenced by measurements from the front door jamb post to the front spindle. Unit construction cars must maintain their original body dimensions. Alterations will be permitted in interest of safety. Unit construction cars must maintain minimum ground clearances. Tire wheelbase must remain the same as manufactured as referenced by measurements from the front door jamb post to the front spindle.

b. Frame modifications are permitted for tire clearance if similar to

frame must be approved for safety and workmanship. Any frame rejected by the NASCAR inspector for being unsafe or showing poor workmanship will not be approved until necessary corrections have been made. A piece of channel iron, minimum 4 inches by ¼ inch, must be installed between the bumper and the rear cross member of the frame by welding to frame rails on each side and bolted with a minimum of four bolts not less than ½ inch diameter, evenly spaced between the frame rails. In lieu of channel iron reinforcement, roll bar cage tubing must be extended to rear of frame rails and connected by welding roll bar tubing cross section to extensions and by spot welding tubing to trunk floor at rear panel. (See diagram rear of Rule Book).

15. SUSPENSIONS

a. Heavy duty springs may be used if similar to original equipment. Rear spring position may be changed, but both springs must be located either inside or outside of frame rails.

b. Sway bars may be reinforced. Additional sway bars permitted.

c. Front end suspensions must be reinforced for safety. Heavy duty spindles and bearings compulsory.

d. Camber: 4° maximum.

e. Wheelbase: AMA specs apply. Standard plus or minus ½ inch. Both front A-frames may be moved forward not more than 1 inch from original position. Left and right must agree. Wheelbase must remain the same as manufactured, as referenced by measurements from front door jamb post to front axle. In case of eligible cars having less than 115" wheelbase, only rear axle assembly can be moved towards rear of frame to conform to minimum 115" wheelbase.

f. Tread, front and rear: AMA specs apply plus or minus not over 1½ inch tolerance on either side to allow for reinforcement of wheels and hubs, measured at center of tire, zero toe-in at spindle height. Steel spacers are permitted to utilize maximum allowable tread width. Spacers must be bolted or welded to brake drum or hub. "A" frames must have a stock appearance. Upper and lower "A" frames may be altered for safety and tire clearance. Lower "A" frames must be the same length and mount in the stock position. Left and right must agree. No offsets permitted.

g. No mechanical or hydraulic device for shifting weight will be permitted inside of driver compartment. No hydraulic weight shifting devices permitted at any time. No weight lowering adjustment permitted on left front wheel during a race.

h. Minimum allowable left side ground clearance 5" on cars with unaltered floor pans and/or relocated frame rails measured at the lowest point of the frame rails, 7½" clearance on cars with altered

side—oil pan, exhaust pipe and flywheel minimum clearance 4". Steering linkage 4" minimum. Cars running at 7½" height must maintain 6" on oil pan and steering linkage, 5" on exhaust. Violation of this rule will subject car to disqualification and/or fine.

16. SHOCKS

a. Heavy duty shock absorbers may be used if similar to original equipment. Use of additional telescope shocks permitted, if similar to original equipment.

b. Air Lifts and coil spring rubber inserts approved by NASCAR permitted.

17. STEERING

a. Tie rods, drag links and component parts must be heavy duty.

b. Interchangeable pitman arms may be used.

c. Center-top of steering post must be padded with at least two inches of resilient material.

d. Racing type steering wheels allowed if approved by NASCAR.

e. No welding permitted on steering parts.

18. BRAKES AND HUB ASSEMBLY

a. Any interchangeable brake and drum assembly may be used. Spot or disc brakes allowed if car is produced with spot brakes as standard equipment. Dual master brake cylinders are recommended. Wheel treads must conform to approved specifications for make and model.

b. Backing plates and drums may be drilled for better air circulation. Scoops may be used for brake cooling, but all scoops must be approved by inspector in charge. Fans, blowers or other attachments will not be permitted. Headlight opening may be used to pick up air for brake cooling. NASCAR approved screens and ducts from the opening to the backing plates must be installed.

19. BODIES

Original dimensions of all bodies must remain as manufactured, except for changes which may be necessary for tire clearance. No lowering of body or frame. In the interest of safety and handling characteristics, a non-adjustable spoiler not exceeding 1½ inches in height may be attached to rear deck lid. An approved spoiler may be mounted to the front underside of cars. The optional non-adjustable front spoiler must be installed a minimum of 3" behind the lower trailing edge of the front bumper and the leading edge of the spoiler cannot extend forward beyond the lower trailing edge of the bumper and cannot extend over 2" below the lowest point of frontal area. Spoiler cannot extend beyond center line of front frame rails. Spoilers must have a minimum ground clearance of 4" except cars at 7½" height must maintain 5" of minimum clearance on the spoiler. All support brackets must be mounted to rear of spoiler—only metal spoilers permitted. All spoilers must be approved by NASCAR before installation.

a. An approved spoiler must be a solid non-adjustable part of the body which controls the flow of air over one surface only.

b. An airfoil must be a permanent part of the automobile body which allows the passage of free air over the top and bottom surfaces of the horizontal plane of the airfoil structure.

When airfoils are approved on the basis of ACCUS eligibility recognition forms, the approved airfoil must fit the NASCAR body templates and can only be adjusted within the manufacturers limits as recorded on the ACCUS eligibility forms. Airfoil adjustments and control are not permitted to be made from the drivers compartment.

c. All cars must have complete bodies, hoods, fenders and bumpers and grilles in top quality condition. No aluminum, light alloys or fiberglass will be permitted as substitutes for steel for any parts of the bodies or bumpers. No homemade grilles permitted. Aluminum and fiberglass trim parts may be approved as replacement parts for die cast parts, but must be approved by the NASCAR Technical Director.

d. Cars must be neat appearing. Head lining and door trim pads must be removed and top panel must be painted. Inside door panel and quarter panels must remain standard, except for approved alterations for roll bar installation. Doors and quarter panels must be covered with aluminum.

e. Floors must be complete and in standard position except for tire inspection; no funnels or air ducts. Engine fire wall must remain standard. Spare tire well may be removed but hole must be covered with metal and welded.

f. Windshields and rear glass must be installed in their original standard positions and standard windshield and rear glass molding must be used and also installed in standard position. Chrome trim or molding must be bolted or pop-riveted in a safe and workmanlike manner. Windshield Safety Clips 3" x 1" x 1/8" must be installed. Three clips bolted to top of car and extending over edge of windshield. Two clips will be bolted to the cowl and extend over bottom edge of windshield. Bottom clips must be visible. Clips must be spaced a minimum of 12" apart. Rear window must be secured with 2 steel straps not less than 1/8" x 1" bolted to roof panel with 5/16" bolts.

g. All doors must be fastened in an approved manner. Steel straps 1/8" x 3" must be welded from the body to the roll bars. Two straps to be welded on front side at hinge locations. Two straps to be welded on the rear side of the door (one) top and (one) bottom. Steel strap 1/8" x 3" must then be welded to the doors so as to match with the previously welded straps and straps bolted with 3/8" bolts. Door handles must be removed and the holes covered with a piece of aluminum only.

h. No streamlining allowed, such as headlights, radiator grilles, top of windshields or under pans. Cars must remain standard in appearance. Grilles cannot be closed.

i. Fenders may not be cut or altered except for wheel or tire clearance which must be approved by NASCAR technical inspector.

j. Hoods must remain in original locked position and closed. Hoods must have original springs and hinges so as to hold up hood when open. All hoods must be locked with 3 pins in hood with attaching cables — one center and left and right.

k. Rear deck lids must have operating original type hinges. Deck lids must be equipped with a self-holding device so as to keep lid up when open. Deck lids must be fastened with 2 pins—one on each side.

l. Any car which fails to fit NASCAR templates or meet body specifications may be required to carry penalty spoiler or smaller carburetor restrictor plate.

20. BUMPERS

a. Cars must be equipped with complete set of bumpers for make and model and must be in top quality condition. Recommended bumper ends should be bolted to fenders as a safety factor.

b. Front bumper — all bumper and lower pan openings must be covered with wire screen mesh only.

21. GLASS

a. Full windshield and rear window in good condition compulsory. Rear window must be permanently closed. No plastic covering. External fastenings on rear window and windshield required. Plastic glass allowed in rear window only, but must be same thickness as original glass, and must be secured with 2 steel straps not less than 1/8'' x 1'' bolted to glass.

b. All side window glass must be removed. No glass or plastic permitted in side window openings at any time.

c. A NASCAR approved nylon window mesh screen must be installed in the driver side window at all tracks one mile and larger and all road race courses. It is recommended that the nylon mesh screen be permanently installed and used at all tracks. (Diagram back of Rule Book).

d. Windshield washers must be of standard production size and type. No hand pumps. No pressure systems.

e. Headlight lenses and sealbeams must be removed and holes covered with flat sheet metal and original headlight and rear light rims must be used.

f. Rear view mirror must not extend outside of car.

22. ROLL BARS

a. Steel roll-over bars are compulsory, and must be approved by NASCAR. Aluminum and other soft metals not permitted. Front and rear roll bars must be connected at top (cage type) and bottom on both sides at seat height. Side roll bars are compulsory and must

extend into door panels (minimum of 4 on left side and 4 on right side) with additional support on the back of the roll bar. Left door side bars must be convex in shape, with some arch. An additional roll bar must be installed across bottom of dashboard, extending from left roll bar leg to right roll bar leg.

b. Roll bars must be welded, and must be not less than 1¾ inches in outside diameter and walls must not be less than .090 inch thick. All welds must have gusset plates, and no less than .090 steel. No pipe fittings allowed. Only round seamless steel tubing permitted.

c. Roll bars must be padded and taped with foam rubber from bottom of left window to center of top in all divisions.

d. For recommended method of installation of roll bars, see diagrams on rear pages of Rule Book.

23. SEATS

a. Rear seat and rear cushions must be removed.

b. Tracks on all adjustable seats must be bolted or welded solid so seat will not shift or loosen on impact. (See diagrams on rear pages of Rule Book).

c. NASCAR approved bucket seats compulsory but must be factory manufactured. Positively no homemade aluminum, plastic or fiberglass seats allowed.

d. NASCAR-approved padded head rest mandatory. (See Safety Regulations).

24. SAFETY BELTS

a. A quick release belt no less than three inches wide is compulsory. Shoulder harness and additional V-type seat belt compulsory.

b. Both ends must be fastened to roll bar cage with aircraft quality bolts, not less than 3/8 inch in diameter.

c. A steel plate may be welded to roll bar cage on right side of driver so the belt can be brought down in such a manner that it will keep driver from sliding from side to side under the belt.

d. The belt must come from behind driver.

25. FUEL AND FUEL CELLS

a. Fuel cells mandatory. Gasoline only as fuel. NASCAR reserves the right to have all cars use the same brand gasoline.

b. Fuel cell maximum capacity 22 gallons, including filler spout. Fuel cell must be encased in a NASCAR approved container (see diagram on rear pages of rule book) of no less than 20 gauge steel, divided into two compartments—a top half and bottom half—whose dimensions are as near equal as possible. Fuel cell must be fitted within the container so that the maximum capacity, including filler spout, will not exceed 22 gallons. Violation of this specification will call for immediate disqualification of car, plus a fine, and confiscation of illegal parts. The following are the only NASCAR approved fuel cell container sizes: 33 x 17 x 9, 31 x 20 x 8⅛, 25 x 25 x 8 1/16, 40 x 14 x 9. Any fuel cells not designed to fit these dimensions must be submitted for NASCAR approval thirty (30) days prior to date of intended use and fuel cell container sizes will be established by the NASCAR Technical director.

(1) Fuel cell and container must be fastened to the floor or recessed as shown in diagram on rear pages of Rule Book.

(2) Fuel cell must be installed as far forward as possible in trunk compartment between frame rails.

(3) Fuel cell, whether installed on trunk floor or in recessed well, must be secured with steel straps, not less than two lengthwise and two crosswise.

(4) When mounting fuel cell through trunk floor an additional container of minimum 20 gauge steel must be welded solid to floor of trunk for installation of fuel cell container. (See diagram on rear pages of Rule Book).

(5) No rags or stuffing permitted to make fuel cell meet 22 gallon capacity. Any materials used to bring fuel cell to 22 gallon capacity must be of steel and welded in.

(6) One 1-inch maximum vent to outside of body at left rear light. (Left hand fill only.) 1-inch drain pipe at filler neck spout. Standard production size filler neck, not to exceed $2\frac{1}{4}$ inches outside diameter. Filler cap must be located in left quarter panel at top of fender line, position approved by NASCAR. Maximum distance from top of filler neck to bottom of fuel cell pan shall not exceed 24". This is the only measurement required for fuel cell body height location and installation.

(7) Either or both right or left side pickup in fuel cell may be used.

(8) All fuel cells must be equipped with removable drain plug; otherwise they will be removed for inspection.

(9) Fire wall of steel not less than 20 gauge thickness must go between trunk and driver.

(10) A rounded pan of 20 gauge steel is mandatory when the fuel cell container hangs down below the frame rails. This pan may be attached to the frame rails only and extend under the fuel cell container, but not beyond the rear frame cross member.

(11) Check valve filler neck inside diameter shall not exceed $2\frac{1}{8}$" maximum. Check valve vent pipe neck inside diameter shall not exceed 1" maximum. Steel balls must be used in check valve assembly. NASCAR Technical Inspectors will reject any previously approved fuel cells, containers, or check valves which are damaged, defective, or do not function properly.

(12) Electric fuel pumps not permitted.

(13) No water cooling permitted on fuel pump.

(14) No additional lines may be used on fuel system.

(15) Fuel lines from cell to carburetor may be relocated to prevent vapor lock, but must remain under floor of car unless otherwise

approved. Line may be replaced with neoprene hose not to exceed $\frac{1}{2}$ inch I.D. Only one fuel line permitted from fuel cell to fuel pump. All fuel lines must be approved by NASCAR. Extra fuel lines or cells, concealed or otherwise, are prohibited.

(16) No pressure system allowed.

(17) Fuel cell vent pipe check valves are compulsory. Check valves and fuel cell must be approved by NASCAR.

(18) Positively no electric motors permitted in trunk compartment.

(19) No icing or cooling of fuel permitted in garage, pit or racing area.

(20) Only two approved eleven (11) gallon fuel cans permitted in pits for refueling. (See diagram on rear pages of Rule Book)

26. WHEELS

a. Wheels must be reinforced. General appearance must not be changed.

b. All four wheels must be same size and diameter and same offset at all times.

c. Hub caps must be removed.

d. Any stock appearing steel hubs may be used.

e. Heavy duty lug bolts must be used.

f. Fifteen or 14 inch diameter wheels permitted, but all four wheels must be same size at all times. Maximum rim width $9\frac{1}{2}$ inches.

27. TIRES

a. No knobs, powergrip baldies, slicks or drag tires permitted. No cross grooving or hand grooving allowed. Standard treads only. Racing rubber permitted.

b. All four tires must be the same size as to actual measurement, and must be of the same make and the same tread design.

c. A measuring device will be used to determine maximum size of tire. Tires cannot exceed maximum side wall measurement of 12.70 inches plus .15 tolerance at 60-pound pressure, mounted on $9\frac{1}{2}$ inch rim. New tires will be selected at each NASCAR event by qualified NASCAR technical inspectors for measurement. Tires to be inspected must be mounted on a 15" wheel having a $9\frac{1}{2}$" rim width. Sixty (60) pounds tire pressure will be required for the measurement.

d. Recaps must be approved by NASCAR, and recaps will not be permitted on any track one mile or over in size. Width of any recap tread cannot exceed the maximum retread width of 11 inches. When retread tires are used, all four tires must be same width and tread design.

e. Same type tread and grade rubber must be available to all contestants. Any deviation from this rule must be approved by the NASCAR Technical Director.

f. Stock racing tires, with inner safety tires, compulsory on all NASCAR super-speedways and other specified tracks. Violation of this rule will result in fine and/or disqualification of the car.

g. Immediately following a qualifying run, wheels and tires from a qualified car will be impounded by NASCAR inspectors and will be returned for remounting when cars are prepared for the start of the race for the purpose of having contestants start a G.N. on the same tires used for qualifying under the following conditions:

(1) Wheels and tires may be taken from all 1st and 2nd day qualifiers and the NASCAR Technical Director is authorized to impound any other wheels and tires he may select. All wheels and tires must be remounted in position from which they were removed.

(2) No contestants will be permitted to make unauthorized tire changes prior to completion of first lap of race.

(3) Contestants requiring or requesting a change of 4 tires will forfeit their qualifying starting positions and qualifying money and will be required to start in the rear of the field.

(4) In the interest of safety, the Technical Director may approve the change of one (1) tire per side without a starting position penalty provided the replacement tire carries the same manufacturer identification as the tire used for qualifying.

(5) Contestants will be permitted to re-balance tires and remount or change safety shields under supervision of NASCAR inspectors.

(6) Tire manufacturers must furnish the NASCAR Technical Director with tire identification markings prior to qualifying and contestants must notify the Technical Director of intended usage of previously approved tires for qualifying runs or in the race.

28. FIRE CONTROL

a. Each car must have built-in fire extinguishing equipment, but it cannot be of the dry powder type—deadline date June 1, 1971. All entrants must have in their pits, at all times, a fully charged fifteen (15) pound capacity dry powder fire extinguisher or its equivalent showing a current inspection certificate.

b. Drivers must, at all times, wear driving suits that effectively cover the body from neck to ankles and wrists. Suits must be manufactured from fire resistant material.

29. IDENTIFICATION

a. Officially issued numbers must be at least eighteen inches high and neatly painted on both sides of the car, and on trunk lid (positioned in center of lid) and facing rear of car. A number 36 inches high must be painted on the roof, reading from the driver's side.

b. Numbers on car and division must correspond with car owner's registration card.

c. Block type numbers, as large as possible, must be on outer headlight and taillight covers.

d. Numerals indicating the cubic inch displacement of engine must be painted on both sides of hood in numerals at least eight inches high.

e. All decals or adhesive-backed emblems supplied by manufacturers for advertising or identification on Competition Touring Sedan race cars are limited in size to the area of a 32 square inch rectangle. Only decals of participating manufacturers will be permitted. Car sponsors or owners names are limited to six (6) inches in height. Slogans will not be permitted. Decal sizes will be determined by multiplying the widest dimension and longest dimension of any decal, regardless of the decal shape. NASCAR reserves the right to assign or restrict the display of decals, identification and advertising on race cars.

30. HELMETS

a. Helmets must be full head coverage type and must meet the American Standards Association Z90.1-1966 testing standards. To be eligible for use in NASCAR competition, the manufacturer of any model helmet must furnish NASCAR with certification that the helmet in question has been tested according to ASA requirements.

SECTION 20A
GRAND AMERICAN DIVISION

International Sedans

Eligibility and specifications as per NASCAR rules supplement covering International Sedan Division available by writing to NASCAR, P.O. Box K, Daytona Beach, Florida 32015.

1. COMPETING MODELS

a. NASCAR Grand American Division races are open to steel bodied 1968, 1969, 1970, 1971 models of American-made and imported passenger cars production Compact or G.A. cars available to the general public. Eligibility of imported cars must be approved by NASCAR before entries are accepted.

b. Eligible 1968, 1969, 1970 and 1971 cars:

American Cars

AMERICAN MOTORS—American, Hornet, Javelin, Javelin AMX

CHEVROLET—Corvair, Chevy II, Camaro, Nova, Nova SS

DODGE—Challenger, Dart, Dart Demon

FORD—Falcon, Maverick, Mustang, Mustang Mach 1, Boss Mustang

MERCURY—Cougar

PLYMOUTH—Valiant, Valiant Duster, Barracuda, Cuda

PONTIAC—Firebird, Firebird Esprit, Firebird Trans Am

c. Eligibility requirements: The specifications for this Division, in essentially the same form as listed here, have been accepted by the Automobile Competition Club of the United States - FIA. The following requirements must be fulfilled in order to establish eligibility under the ACCUS recognition policy:

(1) The 1971 eligible models will be volume production models as selected and approved by ACCUS.

(2) Complete recognition forms must be filed with ACCUS not later than January 15, 1971.

(3) ACCUS will announce eligible models and specifications, recognition subject to verification of minimum production, not later than January 31, 1971.

(4) ACCUS recognition must be granted at least ten (10) days prior to first day of scheduled practice to be eligible for a race. Minimum production must be completed not later than May 15, 1971, along with sufficient information filed with ACCUS to permit ACCUS verification not later than June 1, 1971.

(5) Engines:

(a) Must be an advertised option for the model for which engine will be used.

(b) Deadlines and verifications same as for approval of car models.

(c) Minimum of 500 of each engine must have been produced in car model being recognized.

NOTE: Identical means—Identical in every respect except carburetion, pistons, camshaft profile, and tappets, and which is produced and/or installed by a single Division of a Manufacturer.

(6) Transmission:

Must be listed on the recognition form and approved. No minimum production requirement, but must be an advertised option by the Division of a Manufacturer. Maximum four speeds.

2. ENGINE

a. Displacement—305 cubic inches maximum. (OVERBORING: A total maximum of one cubic inch overbore will be permitted for cylinder wear). Engine displacement may be increased or decreased provided the displacement does not exceed the maximum 305 cubic inches displacement. An engine must be an advertised option for the model in which it was approved.

b. Carburetor(s)—Maximum one four-barrel. Maximum 1 11/16 throttle bore. Holley 4500 series Carburetor not eligible. The approval of any carburetor shall mean approval for all competitors and cost of carburetor shall be a factor of consideration for approval.

c. Cylinder Block — Must be standard production for model engine used, in all respects with the exception of the permissible overbore.

d. Cylinder Head — Must be standard model for engine being used. Limit 2 valves per cylinder.

e. Camshaft — Optional.

f. Pistons — Optional.

g. Crankshaft — Standard production design. Stroke may be increased or decreased.

h. Rocker Arms—Any type except ball or bearing rocker arms not allowed unless standard on engines being used.

i. Valve Lifters — Solid or hydraulic optional. Roller tappets not allowed unless standard on engine being used.

3. LUBRICATION

a. Any oil is permissible.

b. Oil pressure may be regulated at discretion of owner or driver.

c. Any NASCAR approved oil filters and breather caps may be used. This applies to all late model divisions as well as speed trial and record attempts. Dry sump oiling system may be used, but must be NASCAR approved. During running of the race, oil must be added from the engine compartment. The reservoir capacity shall be limited to 1,155 cubic inches and location and installation must be NASCAR approved.

4. ENGINE MOUNTS

a. Motor mounts must be reinforced.

b. Engine may not be moved forward or aft from original position.

c. All motor mounts must be securely bolted.

5. ELECTRICAL

a. Ignition systems must be standard for make and model. Automatic advance in distributor must be in complete working condition. Any make or brand of points may be used. NASCAR approved transistor systems may be used.

b. Any make or brand of spark plugs may be used. This applies to all late model divisions as well as speed trial and record attempts.

c. Batteries must remain under hood as near original standard location as possible and must be standard size for make and model. Alternate battery location must be approved.

d. The generator system must be working within specifications.

e. Self-starter must be in working order. All cars must start under their own power. After race is underway, cars may be started by hand pushing in pit area only, but under no circumstances is any car to be pushed or towed onto race track from pit area. Violation means disqualification.

6. COOLING SYSTEM

a. Water pump impellers may be altered.

b. Removal of fan blades, fan belt or air cleaner not permitted. Any NASCAR approved air cleaners allowed, and they must have the complete element. This applies to all late model divisions as well as speed trial and record attempts.

c. Interchangeable radiator cores are allowed providing they do not alter sheet metal or frame of radiator for make and model. Radiator must remain stock appearing and remain in standard position.

d. Radiator dust screens permitted.

e. Any brand or make of radiator hose or hose clamp permitted.

f. Radiator overflow pipe may be relocated or extended to not more than six feet.

7. TRANSMISSION

a. Standard production, which is cataloged and available through regular dealer channels may be interchanged in any model.

b. All forward gears and reverse gear must be in working order.

c. Drive shaft and universals must be standard production only.

d. It is mandatory that a U-shaped bracket, no less than 2 inches wide and 1/4 inch thick, be placed around the drive shaft and fastened to the floor or cross member of car to prevent drive shaft from becoming dislodged and dropping to race track.

8. CLUTCH & FLYWHEEL

a. High speed clutch assembly permitted as long as flywheel weight is not changed. Aluminum flywheels and clutch assemblies not allowed.

b. Size, weights and material must be normal customer production only.

c. A steel scattershield, not less than 3/8 inch thick, must be installed over flywheel and clutch area. Special production all-steel clutch housings are permitted in lieu of separate scattershields. "Clutch-Flywheel Flexible Housing Safety Shield" is approved for use.

d. Bell Housing — No changes from normal production.

9. REAR AXLE

a. Rear axle ring and pinion may be any gear ratio.

b. Differentials optional. Approved quick change rear ends permitted.

c. Full floating rear axle compulsory, but must not alter tread width or general appearance. Limited slip differential permitted. When limited slip differential is used, one wheel, when jacked up, must turn freely by hand for one full turn—360°.

d. Differential oil coolers, approved by NASCAR, permitted.

10. EXHAUST

a. Muffler must be removed, exhaust manifold optional. Pipes from muffler take-off must be no larger than four inches inside diameter when round exhaust pipe is used. Maximum one 4" pipe per side. Any other system must be approved by NASCAR. Exhaust pipes must extend past driver and to the outer edge of the car, beneath frame, with a minimum ground clearance of four inches. Exhaust pipes must come out side of car in front of rear wheels only.

b. Extra brackets are mandatory.

c. The chief inspector reserves right to reject improperly mounted or unsafe exhaust pipes.

11. BODIES

Original dimensions of all bodies must remain as manufactured, except for changes which may be necessary for tire clearance. No lowering of body or frame. In the interest of safety and handling characteristics, a non-adjustable spoiler not exceeding 6 inches in height may be attached to rear deck lid. Only spoilers listed as available by the automobile manufacturer will be approved, except that an approved spoiler may be mounted to front underside of cars, but 6½ inch minimum ground clearance must be maintained and the spoiler cannot extend outside of the lower fender contour at the mounting position and the maximum width in all cases shall be limited to the car's front wheel tread width center line Spoilers must be mounted below and to rear of the front bumper, minimum of 3 inch set back from lower bumper edge, in a manner which does not change the original frontal appearance, except that original factory spoilers may be approved if mounted in the original manufacturers designated position. All spoilers must be approved by NASCAR before installation. No wings or airfoils permitted whether or not they are manufacturer standard production.

a. All cars must have complete bodies, hoods, fenders and bumpers and grilles in top quality condition. No aluminum, light alloys or fiberglass will be permitted as substitutes for steel for any parts of the bodies or bumpers. No die cast grilles permitted. Aluminum and fiberglass trim parts may be approved as replacement parts for die cast parts, but must be approved by the NASCAR Technical Director.

b. Cars must be neat appearing. Head lining and door trim pads must be removed and top panel must be painted. Inside door panel and quarter panels must remain standard, except for approved alterations for roll bar installation. Doors and quarter panels must be covered with aluminum.

c. Floors must be complete and in standard position except for tire inspection; no funnels or air ducts. Engine fire wall must remain standard. Spare tire well may be removed but hole must be covered with metal and welded. Cars must weigh no less than 3200 pounds. Any weight added to the car must be located within the body shell.

d. Windshields and rear glass must be installed in their original standard positions and standard windshield and rear glass molding must be used and also installed in standard position. Chrome trim or molding must be bolted or pop-riveted in a safe and workmanlike manner. Windshield Safety Clips 3" x 1" x 1/8" must be installed. Three clips bolted to top of car and extending over edge of windshield. Two clips will be bolted to the cowl and extend over bottom edge of windshield. Bottom clips must be visible. Clips must be spaced a minimum of 12" apart. Rear window must be secured with

2 steel straps not less than 1/8" x 1" bolted to roof panel with 5/16" bolts.

e. All doors must be fastened in an approved manner. Steel straps 1/8" x 3" must be welded from the body to the roll bars. Two straps to be welded on front side at hinge locations. Two straps to be welded on the rear side of the door (one) top and (one) bottom. Steel strap 1/8" x 3" must then be welded to the doors so as to match with the previously welded straps and straps bolted with 3/8" bolts. Door handles must be removed and the holes covered with a piece of aluminum only.

f. No streamlining allowed, such as headlights, radiator grilles, top of windshields or under pans. Cars must remain standard in appearance.

g. Fenders may not be cut or altered except for wheel or tire clearance which must be approved by NASCAR technical inspector.

h. Hoods must remain in original locked position and closed. Hoods must have original springs and hinges so as to hold up hood when open. All hoods must be locked with 3 pins in hood with attaching cables—one center and left and right. (See Diagram rear pages of Rule Book.)

i. Rear deck lids must have operating original type hinges. Deck lids must be equipped with a self-holding device so as to keep lid up when open. Deck lids must be fastened with 2 pins—one on each side.

j. Any car which fails to meet body specifications may be required to carry penalty spoiler.

12. FRAMES

Frames may be reinforced, but must remain unaltered in every other respect. Wheelbase must remain the same (plus or minus 1/2" overall) as manufactured in reference to measurement from the front door jamb post to the rear axle. Maximum wheelbase is 112"—minimum 100".

13. SUSPENSION

a. Heavy duty springs may be used if similar to original equipment. It is permissible to relocate the spring towers on Mustangs, Javelins and Cougars in the following manner only:

(1) Front springs may be relocated by building spring mounts into the frame rails so that the springs extend from the bottom side of the frame in the same manner as Galaxie spring mounts. Absolutely no frame changing. The stock frame rails must be used. It is mandatory that the roll bars be extended through the cowl at fender height around the front of the radiator in the same manner as the G. N. Fairlanes. Support bars are to be extended from this bar to support the frame rails—this bar will also serve as an upper mount for the front shocks and for mounting the front fenders. After the

above has been accomplished the inner fender panels can be removed for tire inspection.

(2) Screw Jacks may be used on front and rear suspensions of G. A. cars.

a. Sway bars may be reinforced. Additional sway bars permitted.

b. Heavy duty shock absorbers may be used if similar to original equipment. Alternate shock mounts will be permitted, but only one shock per wheel will be allowed. Additional shocks may be approved for super-speedways.

c. Front end suspensions must be reinforced. NASCAR approved heavy duty spindles and bearings are mandatory.

d. Camber: 4° maximum.

e. Wheelbase: AMA specs apply. Standard plus or minus 1/2 inch. Front A-frames may not be moved from original position. Left and right must agree. Wheelbase must remain the same as manufactured, as referenced by measurements from front door jamb post to front axle.

f. Tread, front and rear: AMA specs apply plus or minus not over one inch tolerance on either side to allow for reinforcement of wheels and hubs, measured at center of tire, zero toe-in at spindle height standard not offset.

g. No mechanical or hydraulic device for shifting weight will be permitted inside of driver compartment. No hydraulic weight shifting devices permitted at any time. No weight lowering adjustment permitted on left front wheel during a race.

h. Minimum of ground clearance of 6½ inches on the left side, measured from the lowest part of frame or body, and not more than 2 inches higher on the right side, measured from the lowest part of frame or body. Oil pan minimum ground clearance 4 inches. Exhaust pipe minimum ground clearance 5 inches; exhaust pipe minimum ground clearance 4 inches. (Use of any special device to obtain minimum ground clearance will subject the car to disqualification because such device may become dislodged while car is in motion, thereby lowering the car below the approved ground clearance.) Violation of this rule will result in fine.

14. STEERING

a. Tie rods, drag links and component parts must be NASCAR approved heavy duty.

b. Interchangeable pitman arms may be used.

c. Center-top of steering post must be padded with at least two inches of resilient material.

15. BRAKES AND HUB ASSEMBLY

a. Any interchangeable brake and drum assembly may be used. Spot or disc brakes allowed if car is produced with spot brakes as standard equipment. Dual master brake cylinders are recommended. Wheel treads must conform to approved specifications for make and model.

qualifiers and the NASCAR Technical Director is authorized to impound any other wheels and tires he may select. All wheels and tires must be remounted in position from which they were removed.

(2) No contestants will be permitted to make unauthorized tire changes prior to completion of first lap of race.

(3) Contestants requiring or requesting a change of 4 tires will forfeit their qualifying starting positions and qualifying money and will be required to start in the rear of the field.

(4) In the interest of safety, the Technical Director may approve the change of one (1) tire per side without a starting position penalty provided the replacement tire carries the same manufacturer identification as the tire used for qualifying.

(5) Contestants will be permitted to re-balance tires and remount or change safety shields under supervision of NASCAR inspectors.

(6) Tire manufacturers must furnish the NASCAR Technical Director with tire identification markings prior to qualifying and contestants must notify the Technical Director of intended usage of previously approved tires for qualifying runs or in the race.

18. FUEL AND FUEL CELLS

a. Fuel cells mandatory. Gasoline only as fuel. NASCAR reserves the right to have all cars use the same brand gasoline.

b. Fuel cell maximum capacity 22 gallons, including filler spout. Fuel cell must be encased in a NASCAR approved container (see diagram on rear pages of rule book) of no less than 20 gauge steel divided into two compartments—a top half and bottom half—whose dimensions are as near equal as possible. Fuel cell must be fitted within the container so that the maximum capacity, including filler spout, will not exceed 22 gallons. Violation of this specification will call for immediate disqualification of car, plus a fine, and confiscation of illegal parts. The following are the only NASCAR approved fuel cell container sizes. 33 x 17 x 9, 31 x 20 x 8⅞, 25 x 25 x 8 1/16, 40 x 14 x 9. Any fuel cell not designed to fit these dimensions must be submitted for NASCAR approval thirty (30) days prior to date of intended use and fuel cell container sizes will be established by the NASCAR Technical Director.

(1) Fuel cell and container must be fastened to the floor or recessed as shown in diagram on rear pages of Rule Book.

(2) Fuel cell must be installed as far forward as possible in trunk compartment between frame and rails.

(3) Fuel cell, whether installed on trunk floor or in recessed well, must be secured with steel straps, not less than two lengthwise and two crosswise.

(4) When mounting fuel cell through trunk floor an additional container of minimum 20 gauge steel must be welded solid to floor

b. Backing plates and drums may be drilled for better air circulation. Scoops may be used for brake cooling, but all scoops must be approved by inspector in charge. Fans, blowers or other attachments will not be permitted.

Headlight opening may be used to pick up air for brake cooling. NASCAR approved screens and ducts from the opening to the backing plates must be installed.

16. WHEELS

a. Wheels must be reinforced and/or approved by NASCAR Technical Director. General appearance must not be changed. Only steel wheels permitted.

b. All four wheels must be same size and diameter at all times. Grand National type wheels permitted. Maximum rim width 8½".

c. Hub caps must be removed.

d. Any stock appearing heavy duty steel hubs may be used.

e. Heavy duty lug bolts must be used.

17. TIRES

a. No knobs, powergrip baldies, slicks or drag tires permitted. No cross grooving allowed. Standard treads only. Racing rubber permitted.

b. All four tires must be the same size as to actual measurement and must be of the same make and the same tread design.

c. A measuring device will be used to determine maximum size of tire. Tires cannot exceed maximum side wall measurement of 11.69 inches plus .16 at 60 pound pressure, mounted on 8½ inch rim. Maximum tread width 10 inches.

d. Recaps must be approved by organizer and recaps will not be permitted on any track one mile or over in size. Width of any recap tread cannot exceed width of original new tread for that tire and the maximum retread width is 11 inches. When retread tires are used, all four tires must be same width and tread design.

e. Same type tread and grade rubber must be available to all contestants. Any deviation from this rule must be approved by the NASCAR Technical Director.

f. Stock racing tires, with inner safety tires, compulsory on all NASCAR super-speedways and other specified tracks. Violation of this rule will result in fine and/or disqualification of the car.

g. Immediately following a qualifying run, wheels and tires from a qualified car will be impounded by NASCAR inspectors and will be returned for remounting when cars are prepared for the start of the race for the purpose of having contestants start a G. A. on the same tires used for qualifying under the following conditions:

(1) Wheels and tires may be taken from all 1st and 2nd day

of trunk for installation of fuel cell container. (See diagram on rear pages of Rule Book)

(5) No rags or stuffing permitted to make fuel cell meet 22 gallon capacity. Any materials used to bring fuel cell to 22 gallon capacity must be of steel and welded in.

(6) One 1-inch maximum vent to outside of body at left rear light. (Left hand fill only.) 1-inch drain pipe at filler neck spout. Standard production size filler neck, not to exceed 2¼ inches outside diameter. Filler cap must be located in left quarter panel at top of fender line, position approved by NASCAR. Maximum distance from top of filler neck to bottom of fuel cell pan shall not exceed 24". This is the only measurement required for fuel cell body height location and installation.

(7) Either or both right or left side pickup in fuel cell may be used.

(8) All fuel cells must be equipped with removable drain plug; otherwise they will be removed for inspection.

(9) Fire wall of steel not less than 20 gauge thickness must go between trunk and driver.

(10) A rounded pan of 20 gauge steel is mandatory when the fuel cell container hangs down below the frame rails. This pan may be attached to the frame rails only and extend under the fuel cell container, but not beyond the rear frame cross member.

(11) Check valve filler neck inside diameter shall not exceed 2⅞" maximum. Check valve vent pipe neck inside diameter shall not exceed 1" maximum. Steel balls must be used in check valve assembly. NASCAR Technical Inspectors will reject any previously approved fuel cells, containers or check valves which are damaged, defective, or do not function properly.

(12) No electric fuel pumps permitted.

(13) No water cooling permitted on fuel pump.

(14) No additional lines may be used on fuel system.

(15) Fuel lines from cell to carburetor may be relocated to prevent vapor lock, but must remain under floor of car unless otherwise approved. Line must be replaced with neoprene hose not to exceed ½ inch I.D. Only one fuel line permitted from fuel cell to fuel pump. All fuel lines must be approved by NASCAR. Extra fuel lines or cells, concealed or otherwise, are prohibited.

(16) No pressure system allowed.

(17) Fuel cell vent pipe check valves are compulsory. Check valves and fuel cell must be approved by NASCAR.

(18) Positively no electric motors permitted in trunk compartment.

(19) No icing or cooling of fuel permitted in garage, pit or racing area.

(20) Only two approved eleven (11) gallon fuel cans permitted in pits for refueling. (See diagram on rear pages of Rule Book)

19. GLASS

a. Full windshield and rear window in good condition compulsory. Rear window must be permanently closed. No plastic covering. External fastenings on rear window and windshield required.

b. Positively no side windows. All cars must have two steel straps not less than 1/8" x 1" on Rear Glass.

b-1 Plastic glass allowed in rear window only, but must be same thickness as original glass, and must be secured with 2 steel straps not less than ⅞" x 1" bolted to glass.

c. Windshield washers must be of standard production size and type. No hand pumps. No pressure systems.

d. Headlight lenses and sealbeams must be removed and holes covered with flat sheet metal and original headlight and rear light rims must be used.

e. Rear view mirror must not extend outside of car.

20. SEATS

a. Rear seat and rear cushions must be removed.

b. Bucket seats compulsory but must be factory manufactured. Positively no homemade aluminum, plastic or fiberglass seats allowed. (See Diagram on rear pages of Rule Book).

c. NASCAR-approved padded head rest mandatory. (See Safety Regulations).

21. SAFETY BELTS

a. A quick release belt no less than three inches wide is compulsory. Shoulder harness and additional V-type seat belt compulsory.

b. Both ends must be fastened to roll bar cage with aircraft quality bolts, not less than 3/8 inch in diameter.

c. A steel plate may be welded to roll bar cage on right side of driver so the belt can be brought down in such a manner that it will keep driver from sliding from side to side under the belt.

d. The belt must come from behind driver.

22. ROLL BARS

a. Steel roll-over bars are compulsory, and must be approved by NASCAR. Aluminum and other soft metals not permitted. Front and rear roll bars must be connected at top (cage type) and bottom on both sides at seat height. Side roll bars are compulsory and must extend into door panels (minimum of 4 on left side and 4 on right side) with additional support on the back of the roll bar. Left door side bars must be convex in shape, with some arch. An additional roll bar must be installed across bottom of dashboard, extending from left roll bar leg to right roll bar leg.

b. Roll bars must be welded, and must be not less than 1¾ inches in outside diameter and walls must not be less than .090 inch thick. All welds must have gusset plates, and no less than .090 steel. No pipe fittings allowed. Only round seamless steel tubing permitted.

c. Roll bars must be padded and taped with foam rubber from bottom of left window to center of top in all divisions. (Recommended installation of roll bars, see diagrams on rear pages of Rule Book.)

23. IDENTIFICATION

a. Officially issued numbers must be at least eighteen inches high and neatly painted on both sides of the car, and on trunk lid, (positioned in center of lid) and facing rear of car. A number 36 inches high must be painted on the roof, reading from the driver's side.

b. Numbers on car and division must correspond with car owner's registration card.

c. All decals or adhesive-backed emblems supplied by manufacturers for advertising or identification on race cars are limited in size to the area of a 32 square inch rectangle. Only decals of participating manufacturers will be permitted. Car sponsors or owners names are limited to six (6) inches in height. Slogans will not be permitted. Decal size will be determined by multiplying the widest dimension and longest dimension of any decal, regardless of the decal shape. NASCAR reserves the right to assign or restrict the display of decals, identification and advertising on race cars.

d. Block type numbers, as large as possible, must be on outer headlight and taillight covers.

24. HELMETS

a. Helmets must be full head coverage type and must meet the American Standards Association Z90.1-1966 testing standards. To be eligible for use in NASCAR competition, the manufacturer of any model helmet must furnish NASCAR with certification that the helmet in question has been tested according to ASA requirements.

25. G.A. DIVISION PIT CREWS

Pit crews in the Grand American Division will be limited to two (2) men over the wall during all pit stops during any G. A. race. No car will be allowed to have any assistance other than two (2) pit crewmen except additional assistance will be permitted to push start cars, but push start assistance must be approved by NASCAR pit officials, and will be limited to a maximum of five (5) men.

SECTION 20B

LATE MODEL SPORTSMAN DIVISION

Open to American automobiles provided they comply with, and adhere to, specifications as outlined for this division.

1. COMPETING MODELS

a. Competition in the Late Model Sportsman division is limited to sedan type automobiles with a steel top (1957 through 1968 models) with a minimum wheelbase of 112 inches and a minimum weight requirement of 9 pounds per cubic inch piston displacement with gas, oil and water (without driver). Cars weighing less than 3,300 pounds, with gas, oil and water (without driver) not eligible. No convertibles, station wagons or pickups allowed.

EFFECTIVE 1972 — 1957, 1958 and 1959 models will not be eligible.

NOTE: When cars are weighed after a race, only water, oil and gas may be added. Wheels and tires cannot be changed, but an amount equal to one (1) per cent of the gross weight will be added for loss in weight due to tire wear.

2. ENGINE

a. Identical engines may be interchanged (Mercury and Ford). Year is optional.

b. No overhead cam engine allowed. No 1963 Chevrolet high performance 427 cubic engine allowed.

c. Following are maximum piston displacements for cars most likely to compete:

1957 thru 1968 Models (Other than 6 cylinders): 430 cubic inches on all engines. .010 for cylinder wear.

(Pacific Coast — 400 cubic inches maximum)

3. HEADS

a. Head may be polished, ported and relieved.
b. Valves may be lightened.
c. Heads may be interchanged in own Mfg. line.
d. High performance heads and approved aluminum heads allowed.
e. Limit: Two valves per cylinder. No valve size restrictions.

4. INTAKE MANIFOLDS

a. Polishing or enlarging port holes in intake manifolds is permissible.
b. Adaptors may be installed to allow proper installation of four-barrel carburetor.
c. Aluminum intake manifolds allowed.
d. High performance intake manifolds allowed.

5. ENGINE EXHAUST SYSTEM

a. Headers recommended on all engines.

b. Exhaust pipes must be properly installed on all cars.

1. Exhaust pipes must extend past driver's compartment and turn out from body just in front of rear wheels.

2. Exhaust pipes may be enlarged. Maximum 4 inches.

6. CARBURETORS

a. Any American manufactured carburetor properly installed will be allowed.

b. Any Holley High Performance Carburetor except the Holley 4500 Series may be used on any make or model.

c. Only one two-barrel, three-barrel or four-barrel factory-made carburetor permitted.

7. ELECTRICAL SYSTEM

a. Any distributor allowed on any manufacturer's line.

b. No magnetos or control spark from cock pit allowed.

c. Dual points allowed in all distributors.

d. NASCAR approved transistor system allowed on all models.

e. Self starter must be in working condition. All cars must start under their own power. After event is under way cars may be hand-pushed to get started but this is to be done in pits only.

f. Batteries must be under hood only. Battery must be as near original position as possible.

8. PISTONS

a. Any piston allowed. Eye brow pistons or pop up pistons may be used in any line.

9. RODS

a. Only NASCAR approved connecting rods will be allowed.

10. CRANKSHAFTS

a. Only NASCAR approved crankshafts will be allowed. Balancing of crankshaft will be allowed and only eight ounces of weight removal will be allowed.

11. CAMSHAFT

a. Any camshaft will be allowed.

12. BORE AND STROKE

a. Cylinder blocks must be production with standard measurement in all respects with the exception of over boring. (Formula for determining cubic inches: Bore x Bore x .7854 x Stroke x number of cylinders equals cubic inch displacement).

13. FLYWHEEL

a. Any flywheel permitted.

b. A steel scattershield, not less than 3/8 inch thick, must be installed over flywheel and clutch area. Special production all-steel clutch housings are permitted in lieu of separate scattershields. "Clutch-Flywheel Flexible Housing Safety Shield" is approved for use.

14. COOLING SYSTEM

a. Fan may be removed.

b. Impellers may be altered on water pump.

15. FUEL AND FUEL CELLS

a. Fuel cells mandatory. Gasoline only as fuel. NASCAR reserves the right to have all cars use the same brand gasoline. Only pump gasoline allowed.

b. Fuel cell maximum capacity 22 gallons, including filler spout. Fuel cell must be encased in a NASCAR approved container (see diagram on rear pages of rule book) of no less than 20 gauge steel divided into two compartments—a top half and bottom half—whose dimensions are as near equal as possible. Fuel cell must be fitted within the container so that the maximum capacity, including filler spout, will not exceed 22 gallons. Violation of this specification will call for immediate disqualification of car, plus a fine, and confiscation of illegal parts. The following are the only NASCAR approved fuel cell container sizes: 33 x 17 x 9, 31 x 20 x 8 1/8, 25 x 25 x 8 1/16, 40 x 14 x 9. Any fuel cells not designed to fit these dimensions must be submitted for NASCAR approval thirty (30) days prior to date of intended use and fuel cell container sizes will be established by the NASCAR Technical director.

(1) Fuel cell and container must be fastened to the floor or recessed as shown in diagram on rear pages of Rule Book.

(2) Fuel cell must be installed as far forward as possible in trunk compartment between frame rails.

(3) Fuel cell, whether installed on trunk floor or in recessed well, must be secured with steel straps, not less than two lengthwise and two crosswise.

(4) When mounting fuel cell through trunk floor an additional container of minimum 20 gauge steel must be welded solid to floor of trunk for installation of fuel cell container. (See diagram on rear pages of Rule Book).

(5) No rags or stuffing permitted to make fuel cell meet 22 gallon capacity. Any materials used to bring fuel cell to 22 gallon capacity must be of steel and welded in.

(6) One 1-inch maximum vent to outside of body at left rear light. (Left hand fill only). 1-inch drain pipe at filler neck spout. Standard production size filler neck, not to exceed 2 1/4 inches outside diameter. Opening in body panel for filler neck must not extend above fender line.

(7) Either or both right or left side pickup in fuel cell may be used.

(8) All fuel cells must be equipped with removable drain plug;

otherwise they will be removed for inspection.

(9) Fire wall of steel not less than 20 gauge thickness must go between trunk and driver.

(10) A rounded pan of 20 gauge steel is mandatory when the fuel cell container hangs down below the frame rails. This pan may be attached to the frame rails only and extend under the fuel cell container, but not beyond the rear frame cross member.

(11) Check valve filler neck inside diameter shall not exceed 2 1/8" maximum. Check valve vent pipe neck inside diameter shall not exceed 1" maximum. Steel balls must be used in check valve assembly. NASCAR Technical Inspectors will reject any previously approved fuel cells, containers, or check valves which are damaged, defective, or do not function properly.

(12) Electric fuel pumps not permitted.

(13) No water cooling permitted on fuel pump.

(14) No additional lines may be used on fuel system.

(15) Fuel lines from cell to carburetor may be relocated to prevent vapor lock, but must remain inside floor of car unless otherwise approved. Line may be replaced with neoprene hose not to exceed 1/2 inch I.D. Only one fuel line permitted from fuel cell to fuel pump. All fuel lines must be approved by NASCAR. Extra fuel lines or cells, concealed or otherwise, are prohibited.

(16) No pressure system allowed.

(17) Fuel cell vent pipe check valves are compulsory. Check valves and fuel cell must be approved by NASCAR.

(18) Positively no electric motors permitted in trunk compartment.

(19) No icing or cooling of fuel permitted in garage, pit or racing area.

16. GAS CANS

a. Only approved gas cans, properly vented, with a flexible hose, and not over 11-gallon capacity. Only two 11-gallon capacity cans permitted in each pit. Filler can capacity must appear in 3-inch painted letters on side of all filler cans. Positively no funnels allowed.

b. Flexible hose must be able to fit snugly over filler neck of gas tank when fuel is being poured in race car.

17. GLASS

a. Windshields and rear glass must be installed in their original standard positions and standard windshield and rear glass molding must be used and also installed in standard position. Chrome trim or molding must be bolted or pop-riveted in a safe and workmanlike manner. Windshield Safety Clips 3" x 1" x 1/8" must be installed. Three clips bolted to top of car and extending over edge of windshield. Two clips will be bolted to the cowl and extend over bottom edge of windshield. Bottom clips must be visible. Clips must be

2 steel straps not less than 1/8" x 1" bolted to roof panel with 5/16" bolts.

b. Headlight lenses must be removed and holes covered with flat metal.

c. Rear view mirror must not extend outside of car.

d. Rear view mirror compulsory.

e. Rear windows optional in regular weekly events, BUT in events at distances 100 miles and more, drivers of cars without rear windows will not receive championship points. When used, rear windows must have complete rear glass or acceptable plastic, with two one-inch metal strips for safety.

f. All side window glass must be removed.

18. BELLY PANS

a. Belly pans not allowed.

b. No streamlining allowed under car at any point.

19. FRAMES

a. Frames are not interchangeable from one manufacturer's line to another.

b. When using older model frames with later model bodies all engines must be mounted in the same position used on the year and model automobile being raced as related to the front axle, regardless of model frame being use.

Measurements will be taken from the center of the rear axle in stock position to rear of the flywheel. This mesurement will be used to determine engine location in year and model automobile being raced.

c. Frames must extend one inch below rocker panels and cannot otherwise be altered except for reinforcement.

d. Frames that are of the I type frame must have an additional frame rail welded between the two original ends to form a box frame. (This I type frame is found in 1958 through 1963 Chevrolets.)

e. Frames must be reinforced for strength.

f. Chevrolet frames and Pontiac frames must have Grand National reinforcement to support roll bars.

g. In lieu of channel iron reinforcement, roll bar cage tubing must be extended to rear of frames rails and connected by welding roll bar tubing cross section to extensions and by spot welding tubing to trunk floor at rear panel. (See diagram rear of Rule Book).

20. WHEELBASE

a. AMA Specifications for make and model apply. Minimum wheelbase 112 inches, plus or minus 1/2 inch. Both front A-frames may be moved forward not more than 1 inch from original position. Left and right must agree. Wheelbase must remain the same as manufactured, as referenced by measurements from front door jamb

b. Tread, front and rear: AMA specs apply plus or minus not over 2 inch tolerance on either side to allow for reinforcement of wheels and hubs, measured at center of tire, zero toe-in at spindle height, standard not offset. Steel spacers are permitted to utilize maximum allowable tread width. Spacers must be bolted or welded to brake drum or hub.

21. STEERING
a. Any approved steering allowed.
b. All tie rod ends, drag links and component parts must be reinforced.
c. Heavy duty steering parts must be used.
d. Interchangeable steering parts allowed.

22. SUSPENSIONS
a. Heavy duty springs may be used if similar to original equipment. Rear spring position may be changed, but both springs must be located either inside or outside of frame rails.
b. Sway bars may be reinforced. Additional sway bars permitted. Heavy duty spindles and bearings compulsory.
c. Front end suspensions must be reinforced for safety.
d. Camber: 4° maximum.
e. "A" frames must have a stock appearance. Upper and lower "A" frames may be altered for safety and tire clearance. Lower "A" frames must be the same length and mount in the stock position. Left and right must agree. No offsets permitted.
f. No mechanical or hydraulic device for shifting weight will be permitted inside of driver compartment. No hydraulic weight shifting devices permitted at any time. No weight lowering adjustment permitted on left front wheel during a race.
g. Minimum allowable left side ground clearance 5" on cars with unaltered floor pans and/or relocated frame rails measured at the lowest point of the frame rails, 7½" clearance on cars with altered floor pans and relocated frame rails measured from the lowest point of cowl and rocker panel and not more than 2" higher on the right side — oil pan, exhaust pipe and flywheel minimum clearance 4". Cars running at 7½" minimum. Steering linkage 5" minimum. Cars running at 7½" height must maintain 6" on oil pan and steering linkage, 5" on exhaust.
h. Violation of this rule will subject car to disqualification and/or fine.

23. REAR AXLES
a. Any gear ratio may be used.
b. Heavy duty rears may be used.
c. Full floating rear axles compulsory.
d. 3/4 Ton truck rears may be used.
e. When 3/4 Ton truck rears are used, hubs must be painted

same color as wheels so spectators will not notice alterations or differences.
f. Quick change center section optional, except Pacific Coast.
g. Differential oil coolers allowed, must be approved by NASCAR.
h. Rear ends may be interchanged in any manufacurer's line.
i. Locked differentials permissible.

24. SHOCKS
a. Heavy duty shocks recommended.
b. Additional shocks may be used.
c. Air lifts and rubber inserts allowed on coil springs.

25. BODIES
a. 1962 thru 1968 intermediate bodies permitted on older model frames. Wheelbase must conform to manufacturer's original equipment.
b. No cutting to lighten body.
c. No fiber glass or aluminum allowed.
d. Upholstery or smooth metal must be on door panel on driver's side.
e. All doors must be fastened in an approved manner. Doors must be bolted with not less than 3/8 inch bolts. (See rear of Rule Book for approved method for bolting doors.)
f. No tunnels or air ducts allowed.
g. Front and rear fenders may be altered for tire clearance only. Full fenders mandatory; no homemade fenders.
h. Complete hood is required. Cannot be altered from standard appearance.
i. Hood must close in original position. Holes may only be bored for cooling in area from leading edge of hood to 5 inches back of leading edge, not to exceed 1/2 inch in diameter.
j. Hood must have positive fasteners, right side, left side and center. Grand National type pin fasteners only.
k. Trunk floors must be complete. When original trunk floor has been removed, it must be replaced with not less than 16 gauge steel and must extend outside frame rails. Must be bolted to frame and quarter panels.
l. Trunk lid must be in operating condition.
m. Grand National type fasteners right side and left side of trunk.
n. All cars must have full floors and fire walls of steel. All sheet metal flooring must be welded and not pop-riveted.

26. BUMPERS
a. Car must have complete set of bumpers in top quality condition.
b. No aluminum bumpers allowed.
c. Bumper ends should be fastened to fenders for safety factor.

27. ROLL BARS

a. Steel roll-over bars are compulsory, and must be approved by NASCAR. Aluminum and other soft metals not permitted. Front and rear roll bars must be connected at top (cage type) and bottom on both sides at seat height. Side roll bars are compulsory and must extend into door panels (minimum of 4 on left side and 4 on right side) with additional support on the back of the roll bar. Left door side bars must be convex in shape, with some arch. An additional roll bar must be installed across bottom of dashboard, extending from left roll bar leg to right roll bar leg.

b. Roll bars must be welded, and must be not less than 1 3/4 inches in outside diameter and walls must not be less than .090 inch thick. All welds must have gusset plates, and no less than .090 steel. No pipe fittings allowed. Only round seamless steel tubing permitted.

c. Roll bars in driver area must be padded and taped with foam rubber from bottom of left window to center of top in all divisions.

d. For recommended method of installation of roll bars, see diagram on rear pages of Rule Book.

28. SEATS

a. Bucket seats are mandatory, but must be factory manufactured and NASCAR approved. Positively no homemade aluminum, plastic or fiberglass seats allowed.

b. NASCAR-approved padded head rest mandatory.

(See diagrams on real pages of Rule Book)

29. SAFETY BELTS

a. A quick release belt no less than three inches wide is compulsory. Shoulder harness and additional V-type seat belt compulsory. Both ends must be fastened to roll bar cage of car with aircraft quality bolts, not less than 3/8 inch in diameter.

b. A steel plate may be welded to roll bar cage on right side of driver so the belt can be brought down in such a manner that it will keep driver from sliding from side to side under the belt.

d. The belt must come from behind driver.

30. HELMETS

a. Helmets must be full head coverage type and must meet the American Standards Association Z90.1-1966 testing standards. To be eligible for use in NASCAR competition, the manufacturer of any model helmet must furnish NASCAR with certification that the helmet in question has been tested according to ASA requirements.

31. SAFETY

a. All cars are subject to a safety inspection.

32. FIRE EXTINGUISHERS

a. Race cars in all divisions of NASCAR must have an approved

33. TRANSMISSIONS

a. Any three speed or four speed allowed.

b. Floor shift conversions may be used.

c. Transmission must work in all gears (No exception).

d. Hydromatic or automatic transmissions not recommended.

34. WHEELS

a. Any NASCAR approved wheel allowed. No dual wheels. No magnesium wheels permitted.

b. All wheels must be of same size, fourteen inch or fifteen inch recommended.

c. Rim width must not exceed nine inches, except on tracks of less than one mile where maximum rim width of 10 inches is permitted. Wheels and tires may not protrude beyond outer edges of fenders.

d. Heavy duty lug bolts must be used.

e. Any offset wheel may be used provided wheels do not extend outside body shell. Fenders may not be altered so as to cover tire.

f. Any steel hub or approved alloy hub allowed. Wheels must be reinforced.

35. TIRES

a. Any NASCAR-approved tire allowed provided it does not exceed maximum side wall measurement of 12.70 inches plus .15 tolerance at 60-pound pressure, mounted on a 9 1/2-inch rim. Measurement must be made with new tire. No knobs or worn out tires allowed. No cross grooving allowed. No smooth tires permitted at start of any event.

b. Recaps allowed on 1/2 mile or shorter tracks.

c. Width of any recap tread cannot exceed width of original new tread for that tire and the maximum retread width is 11 inches. When retread tires are used, all four tires must be same width and tread design.

d. No tire may be protested after running of event.

e. All types of tires must be approved by NASCAR.

f. No racing "slicks" or experimental tires allowed.

36. RADIATOR

a. Any radiator will be permitted, provided hood will close in original position.

b. Only one radiator will be used.

37. FIRE WALLS

a. Only approved fire walls sealing both engine and trunk compartment allowed. Fire walls must not be less than 20 gauge

b. Fire walls must be completely welded on all sides. No soft metal will be allowed.

c. Floor boards must not be removed or cut out.

38. IDENTIFICATION

a. **Officially assigned numbers at least eighteen inches high must be neatly painted on both sides of car, and in 36-inch high numerals on the top, reading from driver's side. Engine displacement and car weight must be painted in 3 inch numerals on right rear side of the hood. Driver's name must be painted in 3 inch letters above the right door.**

b. **Car owner's registration number must correspond with number on car except in events on NASCAR Super-Speedways when special car numbers may be issued by NASCAR. Drivers will not receive points if unauthorized numbers are used.**

c. **Late Model Sportsman cars will be registered by numbers on a state basis only. All numbers will be assigned from NASCAR Headquarters.**

d. **All decals or adhesive-backed emblems supplied by manufacturers for advertising or identification on race cars are limited in size to the area of a 32 square inch rectangle. Only decals of participating manufacturers will be permitted. Car sponsors' or owners' names are limited to six (6) inches in height. Slogans will not be permitted. Decal sizes will be determined by multiplying the widest dimension and longest dimension of any decal, regardless of the decal shape. NASCAR reserves the right to assign or restrict the display of decals, identification and advertising on race cars.**

SECTION 20C
LATE MODEL SPORTSMAN REGULATIONS
(NASCAR SPECIFIED SUPER-SPEEDWAYS)

These regulations are applicable to Daytona International Speedway and other specified super-speedways, and supersede any conflicting rules in this Rule Book in the Late Model Sportsman division. If not covered in these regulations, the Rule Book shall prevail for this type competition.

1. COMPETING MODELS

a. Open to any make or model of American closed car with a factory-made steel top. 1960 through 1968 models eligible.

b. Models with wheelbase of less than 112 inches not eligible. AMA Specifications for make and model apply.

c. Minimum weight requirement for all cars of 9 pounds per cubic inch piston displacement with gas, oil and water (without driver). Cars weighing less than 3,300 pounds with gas, oil and water (without driver) not eligible.

2 ENGINE

a. Engine specifications as listed in the Late Model Sportsman division of this Rule Book EXCEPT that hemi and high riser engines are permitted, but no overhead cam engine or head, or 1963 Chevrolet high performance 427 cubic inch engine allowed. Maximum displacement 430 cubic inches plus 1 cubic inch tolerance.

b. **Carburetor**: Carburetor must be available production model in manufacturer's line. No external alterations permitted.

(1) Rocker arm hemispherical combustion chamber engines restricted to one four-barrel carburetor having 1 11/16 inch throttle bore when used with box-type manifold.

(2) Wedge type engines permitted either single four-barrel, two four-barrel or three two-barrel carburetors with 1 11/16 maximum throttle bore.

(3) Engines with staggered valve design permitted two four-barrel carburetors having 1 11/16 inch throttle bore.

(4) Intake manifolds must be of conventional design readily available to participants. Materials optional.

(5) Fuel injection or superchargers not permitted.

(6) Jets may be any size.

(7) Carburetor restrictor plate must be used when furnished by NASCAR. Only a maximum of three 1/8" thickness gaskets are permitted under any carburetor. Gaskets cannot be altered in any manner.

(8) Heat risers may be blocked.

(9) Any NASCAR approved gasoline filters may be used. This applies to all late model divisions as well as speed trials and record attempts.

3. SUSPENSIONS

a. Front end suspensions must be reinforced for safety. Heavy duty spindles and bearings compulsory. Grand National type Ford front ends may be used, such as spindles, A-frames, steering arms, etc.

b. Steering parts must be Magnafluxed or Dye-Checked. If found defective, they will be confiscated by NASCAR.

c. No floating type transverse springs permitted.

4. WHEELS AND TIRES

a. Cars with wheels over 9 inch rim width will be disqualified and violators will be subject to $500 fine. All four wheels must be of same size.

b. Wheels must be reinforced and approved by NASCAR.

c. Stock racing tires, with inner safety tires, compulsory.

d. All four tires must be of same size as to actual measurement, and must be of same make and tread design.

e. Tires must not protrude beyond outer edges of fenders.

5. OIL COOLERS

a. Approved oil coolers recommended.

6. SAFETY REGULATIONS

a. A quick-release type nylon safety belt of no less than 3 inches width is compulsory. Both ends must be fastened to roll bar cage with aircraft bolts not less than 3/8 inch in diameter. A steel plate may be welded to roll bar cage on right side of the driver so the belt can be brought down in such manner that it will prevent driver from sliding from side to side under the belt. The belt must come from behind the driver.

b. It is recommended that safety belt clasps be secured by locking with tape, twine or a heavy rubber band.

c. Shoulder harness and additional V-type seat belt compulsory.

d. Bucket seats are mandatory, but must be factory manufactured and NASCAR approved. Positively no homemade aluminum, plastic or fiberglass seats allowed.

e. NASCAR-approved padded head rest mandatory.

f. No driver shall compete in any event with head or arm extended outside of a closed body race car.

g. All drivers, car owners or mechanics when running car around track at any time, including warmups, must wear an approved racing type safety helmet and have safety belt and all doors properly fastened.

h. No car shall carry more than one person any time during a race, practice or warmup. A driver shall not permit any person to ride on any part of his car.

i. Race cars in all divisions must have an approved-type fire extinguisher securely mounted within driver's reach, and each pit crew should have an approved-type fire extinguisher with its equipment within ready reach for any emergency.

j. Center-top of steering post must be padded with at least 2 inches of resilient material.

k. Elevated gasoline drums, or refueling towers, will not be allowed. Only approved ventilated gasoline cans, equipped with a flexible filter nozzle and/or tube will be permitted. All cans limited to 11-gallon capacity. Only two 11-gallon capacity cans permitted in each pit. Filler can capacity must appear in 3-inch painted letters on side of all filler cans. POSITIVELY NO FUNNELS PERMITTED.

l. Use of two gasoline cans at the same time while refueling will not be permitted. Violation will mean instant disqualification.

m. Not more than 30 gallons of gasoline per car will be allowed in any pit at any time.

n. When tires are changed on a pit stop, all lug nuts must be replaced and tightened on that stop. Violators will be held in the pits for one lap.

7. GENERAL REGULATIONS

a. All cars are subject to safety inspection at any time before taking part in a sanctioned racemeet, speed trial or special tests, or at discretion of NASCAR officials.

b. Post-Race Inspection — Cars finishing in the first five positions may be torn down after race and inspected.

SECTION 20D

MODIFIED DIVISION

Open to American automobiles provided they comply with, and adhere to, specifications as outlined for this division.

1. COMPETING MODELS

a. Competition in the Modified division open to any make or model sedan type automobile with a factory-made steel top (1935 to 1967 models) with a minimum wheelbase of 109 inches, and a minimum weight requirement of 2,600 pounds with gas, oil, water (without driver).

Wheelbase of less than 109" will be allowed when original frame and body are used for automobiles which AMA specifications list with less than 109" wheelbase, but limited to 1957 to 1967 models. Cars weighing less than 2,600 pounds not eligible. No convertibles, station wagons or pickups allowed.

NOTE: When cars are weighed after a race, only water, oil and gas may be added. Wheels and tires cannot be changed, but an amount equal to one (1) per cent of the gross weight will be added for loss in weight due to tire wear.

2. BODIES

a. All cars must have fenders and running boards if so equipped when new. Nothing may be cut or abbreviated except for clearance or reinforcement. All fenders must cover half of the tire tread. No homemade abbreviated fenders allowed.

b. No car will be allowed to run more than two consecutive race-meets minus any fenders lost in previous competition.

c. All doors must be bolted or welded shut with approved type metal fasteners. No leather straps, ropes, chains or wires allowed. (See diagrams in rear of this Rule Book).

d. At least the top part of hood is compulsory and must be equip-

c. In National championship events, after race is underway, cars may be started by hand-pushing in pit area only, but under no circumstances is any car to be pushed or towed onto race track from pit area. Violation means disqualification.

d. Batteries may be located under hood or floor of car. If located under floor, batteries must be completely encased.

7. EXHAUST

Exhaust pipes must extend 5" past cowl on outside of body.

8. ENGINE

No overhead cam engines permitted unless approved by NASCAR.

a. Blocks may be bored out to any size. NO ALUMINUM BLOCKS PERMITTED.

b. Piston displacement is unlimited. Engines may be interchanged in any manufacturer's line providing car meets all other specifications.

c. Motor may be moved in chassis on all cars, providing the steel fire wall separates the driver's cab from the engine.

d. No overhead valve conversions permitted on stock L-head engines.

e. Any special cylinder head similar to original design permitted.

f. Any stock intake manifold permitted (stock is defined as stock within a manufacturer's line). Any approved intake manifold permitted on small block engines.

g. Only one single 3 or 4 barrel carburetor permitted. Multiple carburetion permitted on small block engines. No fuel injectors or super chargers or Holley 4500 series carburetors permitted.

h. Any type camshaft, valves, valve springs, pistons and connecting rods allowed.

i. Fan and fan belt may be removed.

j. Any type water pump permitted.

9. FUEL AND FUEL CELLS

a. Fuel cells mandatory. Gasoline only as fuel. NASCAR reserves the right to have all cars use the same brand gasoline.

b. Fuel cell maximum capacity 22 gallons, including filler spout. Fuel cell must be encased in a NASCAR approved container (see diagram on rear pages of rule book) of no less than 20 gauge steel, divided into two compartments—a top half and bottom half—whose dimensions are as near equal as possible. Fuel cell must be fitted within the container so that the maximum capacity, including filler spout, will not exceed 22 gallons. Violation of this specification will call for immediate disqualification of car, plus a fine, and confiscation of illegal parts. The following are the only NASCAR approved fuel cell container sizes: 33 x 17 x 9, 31 x 20 x 8⅝, 25 x 25 x 8 1/16, 40 x 14 x 9. Any fuel cells not designed to fit these dimensions

ped with an efficient and safe fastener, plus shock cords. Top part of hood must extend over radiator. On 1949 through 1967 models, complete hood is required and cannot be altered from standard appearance and must close in original position. Holes may only be bored for cooling in area from leading edge to 5 inches back of leading edge, not to exceed ½ inch in diameter.

e. Window openings may be increased to 23 inches maximum.

f. Steel floors must be complete in driver compartment between front and rear fire walls, and must be welded and not pop-riveted. When original trunk floor has been removed, it must be replaced with not less than 16 gauge steel and must extend outside frame rails. Must be bolted to frame and quarter panels.

g. Fire walls are compulsory and must separate driver from engine and gas tank. Fire walls must be steel not less than 20 gauge thickness and securely welded and sealed on top, bottom and sides and must be welded and not pop-riveted.

h. Rear windows may be enlarged only enough to permit entry of spare tires or driver.

i. All bodies must be installed on frame in approved manner. Intermediate bodies up to 1967 permitted on earlier models chassis. When promoters offer a "Late Model Bonus" for bodies from 1955 through 1967, a complete body and complete hood must be used.

3. BRAKES

a. Only hydraulic four-wheel brakes allowed and must be in good working condition.

4. CRASH BARS

a. Any type crash bars will be allowed and all corners or edges must be rounded. Rear crash bars may be only 6 inches higher or 6 inches lower than frame level. Rear crash bumper may not extend beyond the middle of each rear wheel. Front bumper may not be more than 3 inches wider than frame on either side and may not extend more than 6 inches at its longest point from end of the frame. Any inappropriate crash bar will be disallowed, and no snowplow type bumper will be allowed.

5. CLUTCH AND FLYWHEEL

a. No dog clutch or similar design allowed.

b. A steel scattershield, not less than 3/8 inch thick, must be installed over flywheel and clutch area. Special production all-steel clutch housings are permitted in lieu of separate scattershields. "Clutch-Flywheel Flexible Housing Safety Shield" is approved for use.

6. ELECTRICAL

a. Any type ignition system allowed.

b. Self-starter must be in working order. All cars must be able to leave pits and starting line under their own power.

must be submitted for NASCAR approval thirty (30) days prior to date of intended use and fuel cell container sizes will be established by the NASCAR Technical director.

(1) Fuel cell and container must be fastened to the floor or recessed as shown in diagram on rear pages of Rule Book.

(2) Fuel cell must be installed as far forward as possible in trunk compartment between frame rails.

(3) Fuel cell, whether installed on trunk floor or in recessed well, must be secured with steel straps, not less than two lengthwise and two crosswise.

(4) No rags or stuffing permitted to make fuel cell meet 22 gallon capacity. Any materials used to bring fuel cell to 22 gallon capacity must be of steel and welded in.

(5) One 1-inch maximum vent to outside of body at left rear light. (Left hand fill only.) 1-inch drain pipe at filler neck spout. Standard production size filler neck, not to exceed 2¼ inches outside diameter. Opening in body panel for filler neck must not extend above fender line.

(6) Either or both right or left side pickup in fuel cell may be used.

(7) All fuel cells must be equipped with removable drain plug; otherwise they will be removed for inspection.

(8) Fire wall of steel not less than 20 gauge thickness must go between trunk and driver.

(9) A rounded pan of 20 gauge steel is mandatory when the fuel cell container hangs down below the frame rails. This pan may be attached to the frame rails only and extend under the fuel cell container, but not beyond the rear frame cross member.

(10) Check valve filler neck inside diameter shall not exceed 2⅛" maximum. Check valve vent pipe neck inside diameter shall not exceed 1" maximum. Steel balls must be used in check valve assembly. NASCAR Technical Inspectors will reject any previously approved fuel cells, containers, or check valves which are damaged, defective, or do not function properly.

(11) Electric fuel pumps not permitted.

(12) No water cooling permitted on fuel pump.

(13) No additional lines may be used on fuel system.

(14) Fuel lines from carburetor may be relocated to prevent vapor lock, but must remain under floor of car unless otherwise approved. Line may be replaced with neoprene hose not to exceed ½ inch I.D. Only one fuel line permitted from fuel cell to fuel pump. All fuel lines must be approved by NASCAR. Extra fuel lines or cells, concealed or otherwise, are prohibited.

(15) No pressure system allowed.

(16) Fuel cell vent pipe check valves are compulsory. Check valves and fuel cell must be approved by NASCAR.

(17) Positively no electric motors permitted in trunk compartment.

(18) No icing or cooling of fuel permitted in garage, pit or racing area.

10. GLASS

a. Headlights must be removed. Headlight holes must be covered with sheet metal.

b. A safety glass windshield is compulsory on the driver's side with a complete windshield screen on the right side. No plastic glass allowed.

c. Rear view mirrors optional on tracks of less than one mile.

d. All side window glass must be removed.
ATTENTION—REAR WINDOW MUST BE COVERED WHEN REFUELING DURING RACE.

11. RADIATOR

a. Radiator and cooling system may be altered in any way, providing top of hood fits. No auxiliary cooling tanks or radiators - allowed in driver's compartment.

b. When required by track conditions, and on all asphalt tracks, cars must carry catch or overflow tanks of at least one gallon capacity, made of 20 gauge metal and securely mounted as permanent installation, equipped with approved drain cocks. No tin can permitted. Catch or overflow tanks not permitted in driver's compartment.

12. AXLE

a. Locked rears allowed. Floating axles with special hubs permitted. Full floating rear axles compulsory on all tracks. Quick change center sections allowed.

b. No restrictions on axles, shocks, springs, etc., providing ground clearance and height of body not altered. Shock absorbers, by visual reference, must remain within the outline of the body and no holes can be cut in the outer body for the mounting of shocks.

13. SEATS

a. Bucket seats are mandatory, but must be factory manufactured and NASCAR approved. Positively no homemade aluminum, plastic or fiberglass seats allowed.

b. NASCAR-approved padded head rest mandatory.

c. All seat tracks must be bolted or welded so seat is in permanent position. (See diagrams on rear pages of Rule Book.)

14. SAFETY BELTS

a. A quick release belt no less than three inches wide is compulsory. Shoulder harness and additional V-type seat belt compulsory.

b. Both ends must be fastened to roll bar cage of car with aircraft quality bolts, not less than 3/8 inch in diameter.

c. A steel plate must be welded to roll bar cage on right side of driver so the belt can be brought down in such a manner that it will keep driver from sliding from side to side under the belt.

d. The belt must come from behind driver.

15. STEERING

Pitman arms may be changed. No welding allowed on steering parts.

16. SUSPENSION

a. Front or rear suspension must be reinforced.

b. Chassis may be strengthened, but wheelbase must be stock.

c. Lowering of body or frame such as chopping or channeling not allowed.

d. Coil spring front ends may be replaced with straight axles.

e. Minimum ground clearance for oil pan shall be 2" as determined by removing left front wheel and resting brake drum on ground. (Use of any special device to obtain the minimum ground clearance will subject the car to disqualification because such device may become dislodged while car is in motion, thereby lowering the car below the approved ground clearance).

f. POSITIVELY NO MECHANICAL DEVICE ALLOWED IN ORDER FOR DRIVER TO SHIFT WEIGHT WHILE IN MOTION. NO HYDRAULIC WEIGHT SHIFTING DEVICES PERMITTED AT ANY TIME. ANY SCREW JACKS WHICH ARE IN THE INSIDE OF A CAR FOR WEIGHT ADJUSTING MUST HAVE A COVER OVER THE SCREW JACK AND MUST REMAIN SEALED DURING THE RUNNING OF A RACE.

17. TRANSMISSION

a. Any type transmission or differential allowed. Transmissions must be equipped with all forward gears and reverse gear, in good working order.

b. It is mandatory that a U-shaped bracket, no less than 2 inches wide and 1/4 inch thick, be placed around the drive shaft and fastened to the floor or cross member of car to prevent drive shaft from becoming dislodged and dropping to race track.

18. WHEELS

a. Any NASCAR-approved wheel or tire allowed, except that rim width shall not exceed a maximum of 15 inches and tires shall not exceed maximum sidewall measurement of 17.60 inches plus .15 tolerance at 60 pounds pressure mounted on 15 inch rim.

b. On classified super-speedways, heavy duty hubs and spindles are compulsory. All four wheels and rims must be same size. All four tires must be same size as to actual measurements, and must be of same make. Grand National type tires compulsory. No recaps permitted.

19. IDENTIFICATION

a. Officially assigned numbers at least eighteen inches high must be neatly painted on both sides of car, and in 36-inch high numerals on the top, reading from driver's side. Engine displace-

ment and car weight must be painted in 3-inch numerals on right rear side of the hood. Driver's name must be painted in 3-inch letters above the right door.

b. Drivers will not receive points unless car owner's registration number corresponds with number on car. Drivers will not receive points if unauthorized numbers are used.

c. Modified cars will be registered by numbers on a State basis only. All numbers will be assigned from NASCAR headquarters.

d. No solid black or dark blue paint jobs will be permitted — All dark colored cars must have a contrasting light colored top.

e. All decals or adhesive-backed emblems supplied by manufacturers for advertising or identification on race cars are limited in size to the area of a 32 square inch rectangle. Only decals of participating manufacturers will be permitted. Car sponsors' or owners' names are limited to six (6) inches in height. Slogans will not be permitted. Decal sizes will be determined by multiplying the widest dimension and longest dimension of any decal, regardless of the decal shape. NASCAR reserves the right to assign or restrict the display of decals, identification and advertising on race cars.

20. ROLL BARS

a. Steel roll-over bars are compulsory, and must be approved by NASCAR. Aluminum and other soft metals not permitted. Front and rear roll bars must be connected at top (cage type) and bottom on both sides at seat height. Side roll bars are compulsory and must extend into door panels (minimum of 4 on left side and 4 on right side) with additional support on the back of the roll bar. Left door side bars must be convex in shape, with some arch. An additional roll bar must be installed across bottom of dashboard, extending from left roll bar leg to right roll bar leg.

b. Roll bars must be welded, and must be not less than 1 3/4 inches in outside diameter and walls must not be less than .090 inch thick. All welds must have steel gusset plates of not less than .125 of an inch thickness. No pipe fittings allowed. Only round seamless steel tubing permitted.

c. Roll bars in driver area must be padded and taped with foam rubber from bottom of left window to center of top in all divisions.

d. For method of installation of roll bars, see diagrams on rear pages of this Rule Book.

21. HELMETS

a. Helmets must be full head coverage type and must meet the American Standards Association Z90.1-1966 testing standards. To be eligible for use in NASCAR competition, the manufacturer of any model helmet must furnish NASCAR with certification that the helmet in question has been tested according to ASA requirements.

b. NASCAR approved padded head rest mandatory. (See Safety Regulations).

SECTION 20E
HOBBY (AMATEUR) DIVISION
(INCLUDING LATE MODEL HOBBY, CADET AND LIMITED SPORTSMAN CLASSES)

1. EXPLANATION

Hobby division racing is designed to promote greater interest in stock car competition, to enable new and inexperienced drivers and car owners to compete in their own class, and to enable those of moderate means to participate without spending a lot of money for racing equipment.

2. ELIGIBILITY

a. Drivers who have competed in any other NASCAR division are not eligible to compete in the Hobby division, or in the Late Model Hobby and Cadet classes of the Hobby division. Open to amateur drivers only.

b. All Hobby division races, including those in the Late Model Hobby and Cadet classes, are open to American automobiles provided they comply with, and adhere to, specifications as outlined for these events.

c. Hobby Division drivers, including those in the Late Model Hobby class, will be advanced to professional status on notice from NASCAR Headquarters.

3. PROTESTS AND CLAIMING

a. Protests must be registered in the manner detailed in "Appeals and Protests" section of this Rule Book. Officials shall order and/or make inspections at their discretion, but it is recommended that bore and stroke of the leading cars be checked at regular intervals.

b. Each promoter may establish his own claiming regulations, but these must be placed on file at NASCAR Headquarters prior to race meet involved.

4. COMPETING MODELS

a. Any 1936 through 1964 American-made automobiles, including compacts, with a factory-manufactured stock steel top are eligible. Homemade steel tops not permitted.

b. No pick-ups, station wagons, convertibles, or roadsters may race.

5. BODIES

a. All cars must have fenders and running boards if so equipped when new. Nothing may be cut or abbreviated excepting for clearance or reinforcement. All fenders must extend to outer edge of tires. No homemade abbreviated fenders allowed.

b. No car will be allowed to run more than two consecutive race meets minus any fenders lost in previous competition.

c. All doors must be bolted or welded shut with approved type metal fasteners. No leather straps, ropes, chains or wires allowed. (See diagram rear of Rule Book.)

d. At least the top part of hood is compulsory and must be equipped with an efficient and safe fastener, plus shock cords. Top part of hood must not extend over radiator.

e. No reinforcing may be removed from doors. Window openings may be increased to 23 inches maximum.

f. Steel floors must be complete in entire car, and must be welded and not pop-riveted.

g. When original trunk floor has been removed, it must be replaced with not less than 16 gauge steel and must extend outside frame rails. Must be bolted to frame and quarter panels.

h. All bodies must be installed on frame in approved manner.

6. BRAKES

Any four-wheel brakes allowed but must be in good working condition.

7. CRASH BARS

Any type crash bars will be allowed and all corners or edges must be rounded. Rear crash bars may be only 6 inches higher or 6 inches lower than frame level. Rear crash bumper may not extend beyond the middle of each rear wheel. Front bumper may not be more than 3 inches wider than frame on either side and may not extend more than 6 inches at its longest point from end of the frame. Any inappropriate crash bar will be disallowed, and no snowplow type bumper will be allowed.

8. CLUTCH

a. Stock clutch only allowed.

b. A steel scattershield, not less than 3/8 inch thick, must be installed over flywheel and clutch area. Special production all-steel clutch housings are permitted in lieu of separate scattershields. "Clutch-Flywheel Flexible Housing Safety Shield" is approved for use.

9. ELECTRICAL

a. Any type battery ignition is allowed. Magnetos prohibited. Batteries may be located under hood or floor of car. If located under floor, batteries must be completely encased.

b. Self-starter must be in working order. All cars must leave pits and starting line under their own power.

10. EXHAUST

Exhaust pipes must extend past cowl and driver and outside of body. No short stacks allowed.

11. ENGINE

a. Any engine provided it does not exceed 335 cubic inches except that overhead cam engines are not permitted unless approved by NASCAR.

b. Multiple carburetion permitted on flat head engines.

c. Any type camshaft permitted. No roller tappets.

(1) No roller rocker arms permitted.

d. Stock flywheel recommended. Aluminum flywheel permitted.

e. No cutting, machining or lightening on stock flywheel.

f. Only one (1) carburetor permitted on overhead valve engines.

g. Stock fuel pump only.

h. No super chargers or fuel injectors permitted.

i. Special or altered intake manifolds prohibited on V-8 overhead valve engines.

12. FUEL AND FUEL TANKS (Immediate installation of fuel cells recommended.)

a. Any fuel that will mix with water may not be used. No alcohol or alcohol base.

b. Fuel tank must be moved into rear deck space and must be securely fastened in a safe manner on top of the frame, as close to the fire wall as possible. Capacity of tank not to exceed 22 gallons, including filler neck of no more than 2¼ inches outside diameter, mounted on left side. Fuel vent line and filler neck must be equipped with check valve approved by NASCAR. Left hand fill only. No converted grease or oil container or similar utensil may be used as a fuel tank. No funnels allowed. No aluminum tanks of any type permitted.

c. A fire wall must be steel not less than 20-gauge thickness and securely welded and sealed on top, bottom and sides. Fire wall and floor must separate driver from engine and gas tank.

d. Gas lines must run under bottom of body. Neoprene (synthetic rubber) tubing is mandatory for gas line. No glass bowls on fuel pumps. Electric fuel pumps and pressure system prohibited.

e. No rubber hose connection permitted from fuel tank to filler neck. The filler neck must not be fastened to body shell, fender or rear deck lid.

f. Extra tanks, cells, or lines, concealed or otherwise, are prohibited. Only one feed line from tank or cell to fuel pump shall be permitted.

g. Where fuel cells are required, any space filler used to control fuel cell expansion must be a permanent metal spacer, welded in position.

13. GLASS

a. Headlights must be removed. Headlight holes must be covered with metal.

b. A complete safety windshield covering entire windshield opening is mandatory, all other glass must be removed.

c. Rear view mirrors are compulsory, and must not extend outside of body.

d. Rear window may only be enlarged enough to provide for the transportation of tires.

e. All side window glass must be removed.

14. RADIATOR

a. Any type radiator or cooling system may be used providing top of hood fits. No auxiliary cooling tanks or radiators allowed in driver's compartment.

b. When required by track conditions, cars must carry catch or overflow tank of no less than one gallon capacity. Catch or overflow tanks not permitted in driver's compartment.

15. REAR AXLE

a. Floating rear ends compulsory. Quick change rear ends permitted. Quick change center sections allowed.

16. SEATS

a. Bucket seats are mandatory, but must be factory manufactured and NASCAR approved. Positively no homemade aluminum, plastic or fiberglass seats allowed.

b. NASCAR-approved padded head rest mandatory.

c. Tracks on all adjustable seats must be bolted or welded solid so seat will not shift or loosen on impact. (See diagrams on rear pages of Rule Book).

17. SAFETY BELTS

a. A quick release belt no less than three inches wide is compulsory. Shoulder harness and additional V-type seat belt compulsory.

b. Both ends must be fastened to roll bar cage with aircraft quality bolts, not less than 3/8 inch in diameter.

c. A steel plate may be welded to roll bar cage on right side of driver so the belt can be brought down in such a manner that it will keep driver from sliding from side to side under the belt.

d. The belt must come from behind driver.

18. STEERING

Pitman arms may be changed. No welding allowed on steering parts.

19. SUSPENSION

a. Front or rear suspension must be reinforced.

b. Chassis may be strengthened but not altered or cut. Wheelbase and tread must be stock.

c. No lowering of body or frame such as chopping or channeling. Rear cross members may not be altered to drop rear end of car.

d. Minimum of ground clearance of 6½ inches on the left side, measured from the lowest part of frame or body, and not more than 2 inches higher on the right side, measured from the lowest part of frame or body. Oil pan clearance 5 inches. Exhaust pipe clearance 4 inches. (Use of any special device to obtain minimum ground clearance will subject the car to disqualification because such device may become dislodged while car is in motion, thereby lowering the car below the approved ground clearance.)

e. Positively no mechanical device allowed in order for driver to shift weight while in motion. No hydraulic weight shifting devices permitted at any time.

20. TRANSMISSION

a. Only stock transmissions allowed. Must be equipped with all forward gears and reverse gear in good working order.

b. Transmission must remain in original position. Drive shaft must not be altered.

21. WHEELS AND TIRES

a. Any interchangeable passenger car wheels permitted, provided they are reinforced. Must be approved by NASCAR.

b. Heavier hubs and spindles are mandatory.

22. IDENTIFICATION

a. Officially assigned numbers at least eighteen inches high, must be neatly painted on both sides of car, rear deck and roof.

b. Drivers will not receive points unless car owner's registration number corresponds with number on car.

23. ROLL BARS

a. Steel roll-over bars are compulsory, and must be approved by NASCAR. Aluminum and other soft metals not permitted. Front and rear roll bars must be connected at top (cage type) and bottom on both sides at seat height. Side roll bars are compulsory and must extend into door panels (minimum of 4 on left side and 4 on right side) with additional support on the back of the roll bar. Left door side bars must be convex in shape, with some arch. An additional roll bar must be installed across bottom of dashboard, extending from left roll bar leg to right roll bar leg.

b. Roll bars must be welded, and must be not less than 1¾ inches in outside diameter and walls must not be less than .090 inch thick. No pipe fittings allowed. Only round seamless steel tubing permitted. All welds must have steel gusset plates of not less than .125 of an inch thickness.

c. Roll bars in driver area must be padded and taped with foam rubber from bottom of left window to center of top in all divisions.

d. For method of installing roll bars, see diagrams on rear pages of this Rule Book.

24. HELMETS

a. Helmets must be full head coverage type and must meet the American Standards Association Z90.1-1966 testing standards. To be eligible for use in NASCAR competition, the manufacturer of any model helmet must furnish NASCAR with certification that the helmet in question has been tested according to ASA requirements.

Late Model Hobby Class

Late Model Hobby Racing is designed to promote greater interest in stock car competition, to enable new drivers and car owners to compete in their own class. Only Hobby drivers will be permitted to compete in this division. Any driver who has been competing in unsanctioned events and whose status is not clear must make an application for admission to this division. All drivers, car owners, mechanics must be registered members of NASCAR in good standing.

The safety rules and regulations for this Division are the same as for the Late Model Sportsman Division and are covered in another portion of this Rule Book.

1. Competing Models: Open to 1955 thru 1960 models of American made passenger cars.

2. Engines: (No 289 cu. in. or 351 cu. in. Ford engines allowed. No 327 cu. in. Chevrolet engines allowed. Engines must be catalogued for year, make and model).

No overhead cam engines permitted unless approved by NASCAR. No roller rocker arms permitted. No roller tappets or roller cams allowed.

a. Fords: 1955-57 Fords and Mercurys permitted 312 cu. in. engine with overbore of .080 plus .010 for wear.

1958-60 Fords, Mercurys and Edsels permitted 352 cu. in. engine. Overbore .030 plus .010 for wear.

b. Chevrolets: 1955-57 models permitted 283 cu. in. engine with overbore of .080 plus .010 for wear.

1958-60 Chevrolets permitted 348 cu. in. engine. Overbore .030 plus .010 for wear. (The 327 cu. in. engine, heads, intake manifold not legal for Hobby Division.)

c. Plymouths: 1955-57 models permitted 301 cu. in. engine with overbore of .080 plus .010 for wear.

1958-60 Plymouths allowed 350 cu. in. engine with overbore of .030 plus .010 for wear.

d. Pontiacs: 1955-56 models 316.26 cu. in. engine with overbore of .080 plus .010 for wear.

1957 Pontiacs 347 cu. in. engines, .060 overbore, .010 for wear.

1958-59 Pontiacs 370 cu. in. engine, .030 overbore, .010 for wear.

1960 Pontiacs 389 cu. in. engine, .030 overbore, .010 for wear.

3. Carburetor: Only one two-barrel, three-barrel or four-barrel carburetor permitted.

4. Heads, Intake Manifolds: No aluminum heads allowed. Intake manifolds must be cast iron original equipment.

a. Heads on race cars must have same size valves used in make and model. No exceptions.

5. Valves: Must be stock size for make and model of engine.

6. Flywheels: Must be steel. No other alloy allowed. Must weigh minimum of 26 pounds for each model. A steel scattershield, not less than 3/8 inch thick, must be installed over flywheel and clutch area. Special production all-steel clutch housings are permitted in lieu of separate scattershields. "Clutch-Flywheel Flexible Housing Safety Shield" is approved for use.

7. Fuel Pumps: Must be stock for make and model. No electric fuel pumps permitted. GASOLINE ONLY permitted as fuel. (Use of fuel cells recommended). NASCAR-approved fuel vent line and filler neck check valve must be used.

8. Rear Axles: Floater rear end assembly required. Quick change

9. HOBBY must be painted on hood in letters at least 12 inches high.

10. Any driver who shows unusual proficiency in driving may be promoted to the Late Model Sportsman Division at any time.

11. In order to run two heat races there must be a minimum of 12 cars entered. Otherwise there will only be a 20 lap feature race.

12. All parts with identification numbers removed will be illegal.

Cadet Class

The Cadet Class is a part of the Hobby Division and provides training for drivers. Point money in the Cadet class will become part of the Hobby point fund and will be distributed as such.

Competition limited to inexperienced drivers. At the close of the racing season NASCAR will promote drivers showing proficient schooling and the ability to maintain themselves as promising drivers.

PROTESTS, APPEALS AND COMPLAINTS

A. The manner in which Protests and appeals may be made in the Hobby, Late Model Hobby and Cadet classes shall be governed by the NASCAR Rule Book.

B. Protests for alleged violations of rules may be filed by drivers only, and shall be subject to the following conditions:

1. No protest shall be considered unless it is filed in writing with the NASCAR official in charge not more than 15 minutes after completion of the race meet and is accompanied by a cash bond of $100.

2. Protest of a visual violation will not be accepted unless it is filed before the start of the feature event of the racemeet in which the violation is alleged. A visual protest is a protest which does not require any type of measuring device to establish the legality of any part of an automobile.

C. A protest lodged against an alleged violation which is accessible to observations only through the use of tools shall invoke the following conditions:

1. If the protest is not upheld, reasonable expense incurred in inspection shall be deducted from the cash bond posted with the protest.

2. If the protest is upheld, the driver who loses the protest shall be responsible for reasonable expense incurred in inspection and shall not be considered in good standing until that claim has been settled.

3. Only the person filing the protest, the driver of the protested car and other such persons as may be authorized shall be involved.

COMPETING MODELS

Competition open to 1955 through 1964 models of American manufactured hardtop passenger cars, including Falcons, Comets, Chevy II, Dodge Darts, Plymouth Valiants, Plymouth Barracudas, with a

minimum weight requirement of 3,000 pounds. No convertibles, station wagons or pickups allowed.

BODIES

A. All cars must have complete bodies, hoods, fenders, bumpers and be of good appearance and in good mechanical condition.

B. No cars will be allowed to run more than two consecutive race-meets minus fenders lost in previous competition.

C. All doors must be bolted and welded shut with approved type metal fasteners. Window openings may be increased to 23 inches maximum.

D. Floors must be complete in entire car, including trunk. When original trunk floor has been removed, it must be replaced with not less than 16 gauge steel and must extend outside frame rails. Must be bolted to frame and quarter panels.

E. All bodies must be installed on frame in approved manner.

ELECTRICAL SYSTEMS

A. Only stock distributors will be permitted. Distributor cap must be removable.

B. Self-starter must be in working order. All cars must leave pits and starting line under their own power.

C. Batteries must be located under hood as near original position as possible.

ENGINE

A. Standard production engine for make and model. Stock stroke and crankshaft only.

B. 6 cylinder engines permitted. Maximum 300 cu. in. displacement with .010 allowed for wear.

C. Overhead valve V-8 engines will not be permitted. No overhead cam engines permitted unless approved by NASCAR.

D. Cylinder heads must be stock for make and model of car for outside appearance.

E. Stock steel flywheels only; no cutting or altering. A steel scat-tershield, not less than 3/8 inch thick, must be installed over flywheel and clutch area. Special production all-steel clutch housings are permitted in lieu of separate scattershields. "Clutch-Flywheel Flexible Housing Safety Shield" is approved for use.

F. Any type camshaft allowed, except that roller tappets may not be used.

   (1) No roller rocker arms permitted.

G. Single one-barrel, two-barrel, three-barrel or four-barrel carburetor allowed.

H. Any manufactured manifold is permitted and NASCAR approved adaptors for four-barrel carburetors will be permitted.

FUEL and FUEL TANKS (Immediate installation of fuel cells recommended.)

A. Stock fuel pumps only.

B. Only pump gasoline permitted.

C. Fuel tank must be moved into rear deck space and must be securely fastened in a safe manner on top of the frame, as close to the fire wall as possible. Capacity of tank not to exceed 22 gallons, including filler neck of no more than 2¼ inches outside diameter, mounted on left side. Fuel vent line and filler neck must be equipped with check valve approved by NASCAR. Left hand fill only. No converted grease or oil container or similar utensil may be used as a fuel tank. No funnels allowed. No aluminum tanks of any type permitted.

D. Extra tanks, cells or lines, concealed or otherwise, are prohibited. Only one fuel line from tank or cell to fuel pump will be permitted.

E. Where fuel cells are required, any space filler used to control fuel cell expansion must be a permanent metal spacer, welded in position.

F. A steel fire wall is to be used of the following dimensions and construction:

1. Not less than 20 gauge thickness and securely welded and sealed on top, bottom and sides. Fire wall must separate driver from gas tank.

GLASS

A. Headlights must be removed, and holes covered with metal.

B. A safety glass windshield is compulsory.

RADIATOR

Any type radiator may be used provided hood fits in original position.

REAR AXLE

A. Full floating rear ends compulsory. Quick change rear ends allowed. Quick change center sections allowed.

B. Any gear ratio will be permitted.

C. Locked rear ends permitted.

SEATS

A. Rear seat and rear cushions must be removed.

B. Tracks on adjustable seats must be bolted or welded solid so seat will not shift or loosen on impact. (See diagrams on rear pages of Rule Book).

C. Bucket seats are mandatory, but must be factory manufactured and NASCAR approved. Positively no homemade aluminum, plastic or fiberglass seats allowed.

D. NASCAR-approved padded head rest mandatory. (See Safety Regulations).

SAFETY BELTS

A. A quick release belt no less than three inches wide is compulsory. Shoulder harness and additional V-type seat belt compulsory.

B. Both ends must be fastened to roll bar cage with aircraft quality bolts, not less than 3/8 inch in diameter.

C. A steel plate may be welded to roll bar cage on right side of driver so the belt can be brought down in such a manner that it will

keep driver from sliding from side to side under the belt.

D. The belt must come from behind driver.

SUSPENSION

A. Front and rear suspension must be reinforced.

B. Chassis may be strengthened but not altered or cut.

C. Wheelbase: AMA specs apply. Standard plus or minus ½ inch. Left and right must agree. No intentional altering of wheelbase.

D. Tread, front and rear: AMA specs apply plus or minus not over one inch tolerance on either side to allow for reinforcement of wheels and hubs, measured at center of tire, zero toe-in at spindle height, standard not offset.

E. Minimum allowable left side ground clearance 5" on cars with unaltered floor pans and/or relocated frame rails measured at the lowest point of the frame rails. 7½" clearance on cars with altered floor pans and relocated frame rails measured from the lowest point of cowl and rocker panel and not more than 2" higher on the right side—oil pan, exhaust pipe and flywheel minimum clearance 4". Steering linkage 5" minimum. Cars running at 7½" height must maintain 6" on oil pan and steering linkage, 5" on exhaust. (Use of any special device to obtain the minimum ground clearance will subject the car to disqualification because such device may become dislodged while car is in motion, thereby lowering the car below the approved ground clearance.)

F. Positively no mechanical device allowed in order for driver to shift weight while in motion. No hydraulic weight shifting devices permitted at any time.

TRANSMISSION

Any stock transmission will be permitted, and must have all forward gears and reverse gear in good working order, except that four speed (forward) transmissions with floor shift or conversions thereof will not be permitted. Conversions from steering column to floor shift on regular three-speed transmissions will be permitted.

TIRES

A. Any NASCAR-approved tires will be permitted. Treads may be original or recap.

B. All four tires must be the same size.

WHEELS

A. Any NASCAR approved wheel or tire allowed. Wheel rim width must not exceed 8½ inches. Wheel and tire must not extend beyond body shell.

B. All four wheels must be same size and diameter.

ROLL BARS

A. Steel roll-over bars are compulsory, and must be approved by NASCAR. Aluminum and other soft metals not permitted. Front and rear roll bars must be connected at top (cage type) and bottom on both sides at seat height. Side roll bars are compulsory and must extend into door panels (minimum of 4 on left side and 4 on right

APPROVED SEAT INSTALLATION

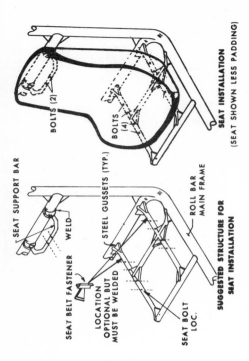

SEAT SUPPORT BAR

SEAT BELT FASTENER   WELD

LOCATION
OPTIONAL BUT
MUST BE WELDED

STEEL GUSSETS (TYP.)

ROLL BAR
MAIN FRAME

SEAT BOLT
LOC.

**SUGGESTED STRUCTURE FOR
SEAT INSTALLATION**

BOLTS (2)

BOLTS
(4)

SEAT INSTALLATION

(SEAT SHOWN LESS PADDING)

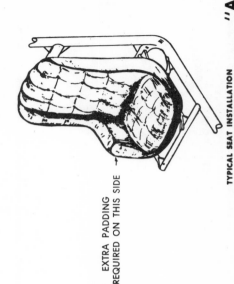

EXTRA PADDING
REQUIRED ON THIS SIDE

TYPICAL SEAT INSTALLATION

"A"

side) with additional support on the back of the roll bar. Left door side bars must be convex in shape, with some arch. An additional roll bar must be installed across bottom of dashboard, extending from left roll bar leg to right roll bar leg.

b. Roll bars must be welded, and must be not less than 1 3/4 inches in outside diameter and walls must not be less than .090 inch thick. No pipe fittings allowed. Only round seamless steel tubing permitted. All welds must have steel gusset plates of not less than .125 of an inch thickness.

c. Roll bars in driver area must be padded and taped with foam rubber from bottom of left window to center of top in all divisions.

d. For method of installing roll bars, see diagrams on rear pages of this Rule Book.

RADIATOR GUARD

Radiator guard must be no wider than frame horn and a height of no more than 18 inches from top of frame horn.

CAR NUMBERS

A. Car numbers must be no less than 18 inches high.

B. On dark colored cars numbers must be white. On light colored cars numbers must be black.

C. Cars must be numbered from 1 to 99—no letters . . figures only.

HELMETS

Helmets must be full head coverage type and must meet the American Standards Association 290.1-1966 testing standards. To be eligible for use in NASCAR competition, the manufacturer of any model helmet must furnish NASCAR with certification that the helmet in question has been tested according to ASA requirements.

SECTION 20F
LIMITED SPORTSMAN CLASS

The limited Sportsman class is a part of the Hobby Division and competition is limited to drivers eligible for the Hobby Division.

Point money in the Limited Sportsman class will be a part of the Hobby point fund and will be distributed as such.

Any deviation from the NASCAR Hobby Division rules must be submitted to NASCAR for approval before they are announced by any track.

All cars competing under Limited Sportsman rules must conform to the Hobby Division Safety rules.

SECTION 20G
OTHER DIVISIONS

NASCAR may promulgate and define special rules and regulations to govern competition on various types of tracks and for different types of programs. Track operators and Chief Stewards will be responsible for the distribution of special rules and regulations to all members concerned.

DOOR BOLTING METHOD

weld to door frame

bolt

weld to main frame upright

Inside view of flange configuration

APPROVED ROLL BAR SETUP FOR ALL STOCK CARS

door bolting flange

four per side

SEAT FRAME

BASE STRUCTURE

four per side
(see above illustration)

ROLL BAR SETUP IN RELATIONSHIP TO X-TYPE CHASSIS "C"

NOTE: steel gussets required at all welds

APPROVED FUEL CELL AND COMPONENTS

CHECK VALVE

FUEL CELL CONTAINER

FUEL CELL

INSIDE DIMENSIONS FOR APPROVED FUEL CELL CONTAINERS.

$9 \times 17 \times 33$, $8\frac{1}{8} \times 20 \times 31$, $8\frac{1}{16} \times 25 \times 25$ AND $9 \times 14 \times 40$

SPECIFICATIONS FOR FUEL CELL AND FILLER NECK PLACEMENT

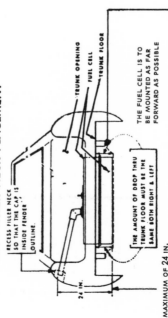

RECESS FILLER NECK SO THAT THE CAP IS INSIDE FENDER OUTLINE.

TRUNK OPENING

FUEL CELL

TRUNK FLOOR

THE FUEL CELL IS TO BE MOUNTED AS FAR FORWARD AS POSSIBLE

THE AMOUNT OF DROP THRU TRUNK FLOOR MUST BE THE SAME BOTH RIGHT & LEFT

24 IN.

A MAXIMUM OF 24 IN. FROM TOP EDGE OF FILLER NECK TO BOTTOM OF FUEL CELL WILL BE ALLOWED

POSITIVELY NO ELECTRIC MOTORS ALLOWED IN THE TRUNK

Container for Fuel Cell to Mount In-Welded Solid to Floor Pan

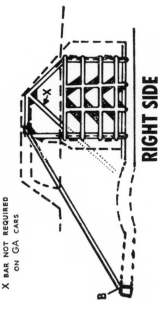

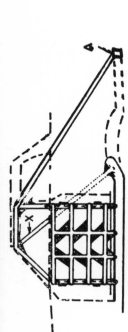

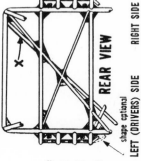

ISOMETRIC VIEW OF STRUCTURE

GUSSETS REQUIRED AT ALL WELDS

X=REFERENCED ON PAGES C & D

APPROVED NYLON MESH SCREEN
Attached to Roll Bar with
Hose Clamps

Rear Upright Roll Bar

Hole Drilled in Roll Bar For Steel Rod

Roof Line Roll Bar

3/8" Steel Rod

Top Side Bar in Left Door

Stock Seat Belt—Male End Attached to Top Roll Bar — Attach other end to Net around Steel Rod, so as to adjust Net tight.

"E"

LEFT (DRIVER'S) SIDE

X BAR NOT REQUIRED ON GA CARS

RIGHT SIDE

A and B extended to rear of frame rails and connected by welding roll bar cross section to extensions and spot welding cross bar tubing to floor of trunk at the rear panel.

"D"

REAR VIEW

LEFT (DRIVERS) SIDE   RIGHT SIDE

shape optional

NOTE: all welds on roll bars must have steel gusset plates.

National Stock Car Racing Commission

RUSS MOYER, Chairman
ART ATKINSON
BILL AMICK
BOB BARKHIMER
JOHN BRUNER, SR.
BILL GAZAWAY

PHIL HOLMER
PETE KELLER
CARLETON MERRILL
RALPH OUDERKIRK
KEN PIPER
LES RICHTER

BOB SALL

Address all communications:

P.O. Box K
Daytona Beach, Fla. 32015

PHONE
(904) 253-0611

APPROVED REFUELING CAN

MAXIMUM CAPACITY 11 GALLONS

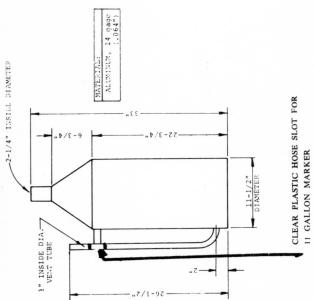

MATERIAL: ALUMINUM, 14 gage (.064")

2-1/4" INSIDE DIAMETER

6-3/4"

22-3/4"

33"

1" INSIDE DIA. VENT TUBE

11-1/2" DIAMETER

26-1/2"

2"

CLEAR PLASTIC HOSE SLOT FOR 11 GALLON MARKER

"F"